Reading Attainment System

Book 2

by Caleb E. Crowell &
Donn Mosenfelder

Illustrations by Edgar Blakeney

EDUCATIONAL DESIGN, INC.   **EDI 282**

ISBN# 0-87694-051-3   EDI 282

To the Reader:

The stories in this book are on many different topics. We hope you will find them interesting to read. These stories, and the exercises that go with them, aim at helping you improve your reading, vocabulary, and thinking skills.

Each story starts with a sentence or two above the picture to help you understand what you are about to read.

A glossary lists and explains the hard words within the story. You will find this glossary at the top of the second page of the story.

Following each story are three sets of exercises:

Reading Skills Exercises will test your understanding of what you have read.

Vocabulary Skills Exercises will give you a chance to improve your understanding of key words in the story.

Thinking Skills Exercises will ask you to use information you have learned to answer questions which require a lot of thought and reasoning.

Table of Contents

There are many different kinds of musical instruments in the world. You know the piano, the guitar, the drum, and many others. But here are some really strange instruments you may never have heard of!

1. The Strangest Musical Instruments in the World

1   What is the strangest musical instrument in the world?

2   Some instruments are strange because they are so big. Someone once made a 10-foot-long guitar. It weighed 300 pounds. Someone else made a string bass 14 feet tall. That's almost as tall as a two-story house.

3   It took three people to make a giant harp that was 13½ feet tall. They couldn't use ordinary harp strings on it. They had to use aircraft cables.

4   All marching bands contain a kind of big horn called a tuba. The biggest tuba ever made is 39 feet long. Of course, the tube of a tuba is coiled up. So the giant tuba really stands only 7½ feet high. That's a foot and a half taller than the man who plays it.

5   The longest horn of all is not coiled up. It is a kind of horn played by the people who live in the Alps Mountains of Europe, and so it is called an alphorn. Ordinary alphorns are more than 10 feet long. The biggest one is a real giant. It stretches more than 78 feet.

GLOSSARY

bass	An instrument that plays low (or **bass**) notes. *Example:* The string bass was replaced in rock bands by a bass guitar.
cables	Ropes made of wire. *Example:* Airplane cables control many of the moving parts on an airplane.
guitar	The main instrument in most rock bands, and other instruments related to it. *Example:* Rock players play an electric guitar, but in Spain and South America most guitars are not electric.
keyboard	A set of keys on a musical instrument, like those on a piano. You press them to play the instrument. *Example:* A piano is a keyboard instrument.
spiritual	Holy or sacred in a religion. *Example:* Ministers and priests are spiritual leaders.

6   What about instruments that are strange because they are small? One man has made a violin that is two inches long. That is about the size of a large bug. The amazing thing is that the man who made this violin is able to play it.

7   It is not just size that can make an instrument strange. For example, take the nose flute. The nose flute is played in the Pacific islands. As you can tell from its name, you play it with your nose. You can't blow very hard with your nose, of course. So the nose flute is not very loud. But the people who play it think that nose breath has spiritual powers. They think it is perfect for making music.

8   Have you ever heard of a musical saw? It looks like an ordinary saw. You play it by drawing a bow across its back edge. You bend the saw back and forth to make the different notes. It's not as dangerous as it looks. The saw isn't sharp.

9   But the strangest instrument of all time was one invented 500 years ago. It was invented to amuse a king of France, who was visiting one of his lords. It was a row of pigs!

10   Each pig had a different squeal. The inventor lined up all the pigs in order, from low squeal to high squeal. He also made a keyboard like the one on a piano. Hitting a key made a stick poke a pig. This made the pig squeal.

11   The king was able to recognize the tunes played on the poor pigs. He was delighted. The pigs were not delighted at all. And after the king left, the strangest musical instrument in the world was never played again.

Reading Skills BOOK 2
SELECTION 1

1. The story tells about some instruments

   a. that are very big
   b. that cost a lot
   c. that no one could play

2. The giant string bass was

   a. 10 feet tall
   b. 14 feet tall
   c. 300 feet tall

3. The instrument that uses aircraft cables for strings is

   a. a guitar
   b. a harp
   c. a string bass

4. The instrument named after a mountain range is

   a. the alphorn
   b. the guitar
   c. the tuba

5. (Paragraph 7) Pacific islanders play the nose flute because

   a. it is very loud, and they like loud music
   b. they have very long noses
   c. they think nose breath is sacred, and good for music

6. (Paragraph 8) You play a musical saw with

   a. drum sticks
   b. a keyboard
   c. a violin bow

7. (Paragraph 9) The strangest instrument of all was

   a. a giant flute
   b. a group of pigs
   c. a king of France

8. The strangest instrument was played with

   a. drum sticks
   b. a keyboard
   c. a violin bow

9. How many times was the strangest instrument played in public?

   a. once
   b. three times
   c. 30 times

10. The king of France probably thought that the music of the pigs was

   a. very beautiful
   b. very funny
   c. very old

Vocabulary Skills BOOK 2 SELECTION 1

Glossary Check. Find the Glossary word that should go in each sentence. Then write the word.

1. Many of our biggest bridges are held up by steel _____.

2. You take the high part, and I'll sing _____.

Word Meanings. The meaning of a word depends on how the word is used.

3. Paragraph 2 says:
   "That's almost as tall as a two-story house."

   In this sentence, what does **story** mean?

   a. floor
   b. lie
   c. tale

4. Paragraph 4 says:
   "All marching bands contain a kind of big horn."

   In this sentence, what does **horn** mean?

   a. beeper on a car
   b. sharp things on an animal's head
   c. something you blow into to make music

5. Paragraph 5 says:
   "It stretches more than 78 feet."

   In this sentence, what does **stretches** mean?

   a. extends
   b. is pulled out like a rubber band
   c. pulls on its muscles

6. Paragraph 8 says:

"You play it by drawing a bow across its back edge."

In this sentence, what does **bow** mean?

a. bending over at the waist
b. thing you shoot an arrow with
c. thing you use to play a violin with

7. Paragraph 8 says:

"You bend the saw back and forth to make the different notes."

In this sentence, what does **notes** mean?

a. jots down on a piece of paper
b. musical sounds
c. short written messages

8. Paragraph 11 says:

"The pigs were not delighted at all."

This time, write the word that means the opposite of **disappointed**.

Alphabetical Order. To put words in alphabetical, or a-b-c order, look at the first letters of the words. These words are in alphabetical order:

1. back	2. may	3. today
car	might	took
full	more	town

9. Which word would you put next after the word **instrument**?

a. guitar
b. horn
c. violin

10. Look again at the words in question 9. Which word would you put next after the word **harp**?

Thinking Skills BOOK 2 SELECTION 1

Correct Order. Putting things in correct order is an important thinking skill.

1. Look at the list below. Put the items in order of <u>length</u>, from longest to shortest.
   (1 = longest, 2 = second longest, 3 = shortest)

   a. ____ longest alphorn
   b. ____ longest tuba
   c. ____ nose flute

2. Look at the list. Put the items in order of <u>height</u>, from tallest to shortest.

   a. ___ largest guitar
   b. ___ largest harp
   c. ___ largest string bass

3. Look at the list. Put the items in order of <u>strangeness</u>, from least strange to most strange.
   (1 = least strange, 2 = somewhat strange, 3 = very strange)

   a. ___ musical pigs
   b. ___ musical saw
   c. ___ violin

Cause and Effect. Look at these two sentences:

   Billie told a joke. Everybody laughed.

Telling a joke caused everybody to laugh. The telling is the **cause**. Everybody laughing is the **effect**. We say that the two sentences show a **cause-effect** relationship.

4. Check the pair of sentences below that have a cause-effect relationship in the story. (The first is the reason for the second, or causes the second.)

   a. Alphorns are more than 10 feet long. The biggest stretches more than 78 feet.
   b. Draw a bow across a musical saw. A note sounds.
   c. The smallest violin was two inches long. The man who made it could play it.

5. Again, check the pair that have a cause-effect relationship.

   a. The nose flute is played in the Pacific islands. You play it with your nose.
   b. One strange instrument was invented 400 years ago. It was invented for a king of France.
   c. Hitting a key made a stick poke a pig. The pig squealed.

All throughout history, there have been people who say that the world is about to end. Usually no one believes them. But what happens when some people <u>do</u> believe that the world is coming to an end?

2. The End of the World

1   In February, 1761, an earthquake hit London, England. A month later, a quake hit again. Neither quake did much harm.

2   But earthquakes are very rare in England. And these quakes happened exactly four weeks apart. A soldier named William Bell decided that the quakes were a warning. They meant that the earth was coming to an end. It would end exactly four weeks after the second quake.

3   Bell made speech after speech warning the people of London. Panic spread. Londoners left London in huge numbers. Some escaped in boats. Some fled to the country.

4   Many Londoners didn't believe Bell. They pointed out that if the whole world was going to end, it was no safer to leave London than to stay there. But frightened Londoners still fled. Finally the awful day came.

5   Nothing happened.

```
┌─ GLOSSARY ──────────────────────────────────────────┐
```

century	100 years. *Example:* The United States won its freedom more than two centuries ago.
earthquake or quake	A shaking of the ground. *Example:* The earthquake knocked over the houses.
fled	Ran away in fear. (It is a form of the word *flee*, which means "to run away in fear.") *Example:* The robber fled from the policeman.
panic	Great fear. *Example:* The forest fire caused the animals to run away in panic.
predict	To tell what will happen in the future. *Example:* The doctor predicted I would get better.
prophet	Someone who predicts things. *Example:* Daniel was a prophet in the Bible.

6 It was not the first time that Londoners had left London to get away from the end of the world. More than 200 years earlier, a group of prophets made the same prediction. They said that the world would end on February 1, 1524. People fled, just as they did two and a half centuries later. When February 1 came and went, the prophets checked their numbers. They found a small mistake. They then said that the world would end in 1624, not 1524.

7 On February 1, 1624, nothing happened either.

8 Predictions about the end of the world keep popping up. Several times in the 1840's, followers of a New England prophet waited for the end of the world. After the end failed to come four times in a row, most of the prophet's followers left him.

9 In 1925 a young California woman predicted that an angel was about to bring the world to an end. Reporters went with her and her followers to the top of a hill to wait for the angel. When nothing happened, the woman blamed the reporters. She said that their cameras annoyed the angel. And so the angel didn't come.

10 One prophet of the end of the world was a man named Wilbur Glenn Voliva. Voliva believed a lot of strange things. He belived that the earth is flat. He also believed he would live to the age of 120 by eating nuts and drinking milk. He used to say, "I never met anyone who knew close to as much on any subject as I do." He predicted the end of the world in 1923, 1927, 1930, and 1940. Even when nothing happened, it never occurred to him that he could be wrong.

11   So far, the world hasn't ended. But the prophets keep trying. One has predicted that the world will end in the year 2000. He says that a black rainbow will suck up all the air.

Reading Skills BOOK 2
SELECTION 2

1. What was the result of the earthquake of 1761?

   a. London was destroyed
   b. London was rebuilt
   c. people fled from London

2. How did Bell spread his warning?

   a. he made many speeches
   b. he told a few friends
   c. he wrote to newspapers

3. When in 1761 did the **second** earthquake hit London?

   a. February
   b. March
   c. April

4. Bell said the earth would come to an end in

   a. February
   b. March
   c. April

5. (Paragraph 6) When nothing happened on February 1, 1524, what did the fortune tellers say?

   a. the cameras scared an angel
   b. they had saved London
   c. they made a mistake in their math

6. (Paragraph 9) The world did not end in 1925. How did a leader of the 1925 group explain this?

   a. he said the angel couldn't find the right hilltop
   b. he said the angel didn't like reporters
   c. he said the angel's math was wrong

7. (Paragraph 10) Wilbur Glenn Voliva believed that

   a. the earth was flat
   b. the moon is made of green cheese
   c. he would live forever

8. (Paragraph 11) One prophet says that in the year 2000 the end of the world will be caused by

    a. a black rainbow
    b. a comet
    c. a great flood

9. What probably happened when the world didn't end in 1761?

    a. the people believed it would end in 1762
    b. the people left in London also fled
    c. the people who had fled went back home

10. Do you think that the writer of this story believes that the world will end in the year 2000?

    a. yes
    b. no
    c. can't tell

Vocabulary Skills BOOK 2 SELECTION 2

Glossary Check. Find the Glossary word that should go in each sentence. Then write the word.

1. I cannot _____ what the general will do when he hears that the army has been destroyed.

2. _____ swept through the crowd when the monster approached.

Word Meanings. The meaning of a word depends on how the word is used.

3. Paragraph 4 says:
   "Finally the awful day came."

   In this sentence, what does *awful* mean?

    a. bad-tasting
    b. frightening
    c. stormy and rainy

4. Paragraph 6 says:
   "The prophets checked their numbers."

   In this sentence, what does *checked* mean?

    a. put a check mark beside
    b. looked at again carefully
    c. put away safely

5. Paragraph 9 says:

"An angel was about to bring the world to an end."

In this sentence, what does **angel** mean?

a. beautiful and pure young woman
b. messenger from Heaven
c. person who backs a play

6. Paragraph 1 says:

"Neither quake did much harm."

Write the word that means **damage**.

7. Paragraph 6 says:

"They found a small mistake."

Write the word that means **error**.

8. Paragraph 9 says:

"She said that their cameras annoyed the angel."

This time, write the word that means the opposite of **pleased**.

Using Apostrophes. The meaning of a word or a sentence may depend on how an apostrophe is used.

9. Paragraph 2 says: "It was not the first time that Londoners had left London."

What is another way to write "**It was not**"?

a. It isn't
b. It wasn't
c. It won't

10. Paragraph 4 says: "Many Londoners didn't believe Bell."

What is another way to write "**didn't**"?

a. did'nt
b. did not
c. don't

Thinking Skills BOOK 2 SELECTION 2

Fact and Opinion. In your thinking, you should be able to tell a fact from an opinion.

"The sun is a star" is a **fact**. It can be proved by a scientist.
"George Washington was a great president" is an **opinion**. It may be a good opinion, but it's not something a scientist can prove.

1. Which of these statements states a *fact*? (choose one)

   a. Earthquakes may predict the end of the world.
   b. Fortune tellers are always fakes.
   c. The earthquakes of 1761 did not damage London much.

2. Which of these statements states an *opinion*? (choose one)

   a. Earthquakes are rare in England.
   b. It is silly to believe that a black rainbow will suck up the air.
   c. Voliva was wrong when he predicted the end of the world in 1927.

Logical Thinking. Thinking logically means taking information and drawing the right conclusions from it.

3. Look at these statements:

   Earthquakes are unusual in England.
   Earthquakes hit England in February, 1761.

   Which conclusion is correct?

   a. Earthquakes have become usual in England.
   b. Something unusual happened in England in February, 1761.
   c. The world was coming to an end.

4. Look at these statements. (Pretend that the first one is true.)

   The world will be destroyed in 1761.
   Both London and the countryside around it are part of the world.

   Which conclusion is correct?

   a. London is a safe place to be in 1761.
   b. Both London and the countryside will be destroyed in 1761.
   c. To be safe in 1761, get out of London and go to the countryside.

5. Look at these statements:

   All big cities contain some people with strange ideas.
   London is a big city.

   Which conclusion is correct?

   a. London contains some people with strange ideas.
   b. Londoners all have strange ideas.
   c. The ideas of Londoners are strange.

The true story of the train wreck that gave rise to one of the most famous of all American songs.

3. Who Was the Real Casey Jones?

1   It was a dark spring night, April 30, 1900. A fast train was making a run south to New Orleans. It was the Illinois Central's mail train, "the Cannonball."

2   The run should have been easy. But there was one thing the train's engineer did not know. Ahead of him there was a slow freight train. And the two trains were on the same track.

3   The freight train should have switched to a side line. But that night it broke down. And the Cannonball was going too fast.

4   In any case, the Cannonball caught up with the freight. At 75 miles an hour, the Cannonball could not stop. It smashed into the back of the freight. And the engineer was killed.

5   The tale of the wreck might have been forgotten. But it wasn't. It is now one of the best-known wrecks in our history.

6   The engineer on the fast mail train was a man named John Luther Jones. Jones had grown up in Cayce, Kentucky. He got his nickname from the name of his home town. His friends called him "Casey" Jones.

7   Jones was well liked. He was respected. He was a good engineer. People said he died the death of a real railroad man.

┌─ **GLOSSARY** ─────────────────────────────────┐

engineer   A person who runs a train.
                 Example: The engineer stopped the train to let a cow
                 cross the tracks.

freight   Things shipped from one place to another.
                 Example: The train carried fruit, meat, machine
                 parts, and other freight.

nickname   A short or special name that your friends call you.
                 Example: A left-handed man may be given the nick-
                 name "Lefty."

respect   Look up to.
                 Example: People respect someone who does a
                 tough job well.

└──┘

8   People began to tell stories about Casey Jones. Men who had not known him when he was alive heard of him and his death.

9   One of these men was named T. Lawrence Seibert. In 1909, he wrote the words to a song about Jones. This song was called "Casey Jones." It is still sung today.

10 Most of the facts in Seibert's song are wrong. For one thing, the song says that Casey was taking the mail to San Francisco. And it says that the trains crashed head-on.

11 Then, too, the song adds things that Seibert may have made up himself. It says that the train was eight hours late. So it had to go at top speed to make up time. In the song, Casey tells the fireman that the mail will get to San Francisco. But he somehow knows the trip will kill him.

12 But it's a good song in any case. A lot of railroad men have sung it and loved it. So have a lot of other people.

13 The song is sung all over our land. But the words and the tune change in each part of the country. The facts of the wreck don't seem to matter much now.

14 Few people today have heard of the real John Luther Jones. But Casey Jones is known by millions.

Reading Skills BOOK 2 SELECTION 3

1. This is a story about

   a. a baseball player named Casey
   b. a train engineer named Casey
   c. a train named "The Casey"

2. Who wrote the song "Casey Jones"?

   a. a man named John Luther Jones
   b. a man named T. Lawrence Seibert
   c. no one wrote it—it's a folk song

3. Casey Jones got his nickname because

   a. he grew up in Cayce, Kentucky
   b. he grew up in Kansas City, Missouri
   c. he was an Irishman named Casey

4. (Paragraph 1) What was the Cannonball carrying?

   a. freight
   b. mail
   c. passengers

5. (Paragraph 4) How did the wreck happen?

   a. the Cannonball hit the back of the freight
   b. the freight and the Cannonball met head on
   c. the freight hit the back of the Cannonball

6. (Paragraphs 8 and 9) What did Seibert know about the real Casey Jones?

   a. he heard the story of Casey's death
   b. he knew Casey
   c. he saw the wreck take place

7. When he was killed, the real Casey Jones was going

   a. to Illinois
   b. to New Orleans
   c. to San Francisco

8. The song, "Casey Jones" says that

    a. the Cannonball was eight hours late
    b. Casey jumped off the train before it crashed
    c. Casey lived for years after the crash

9. In the song, Casey says that the trip will kill him. Why do you think Seibert put that in the song?

    a. the real Casey Jones wanted to kill himself
    b. the real Casey Jones was afraid
    c. Seibert thought it would make the song better

10. Why is Casey Jones known today by millions?

    a. millions of people met him
    b. millions of people read about the wreck
    c. the song made him famous

Vocabulary Skills BOOK 2 SELECTION 3

Glossary Check. Find the Glossary word that should go in each sentence. Then write the word.

1. Her real name was Della, but "Red" was her _____.

2. If you act like a fool, you won't win anyone's _____.

Word Meanings. The meaning of a word depends on how the word is used.

3. Paragraph 1 says:
    "A fast train was making a run south to New Orleans."

    In this sentence, what does *run* mean?
    a. go very fast
    b. race
    c. trip

4. Paragraph 3 says:
    "The freight train should have switched to a side line."

    In this sentence, what does *line* mean?
    a. mark
    b. rope
    c. track

5. Paragraph 5 says:

"The tale of the wreck might have been forgotten."

In this sentence, what does *tale* mean?
a. end
b. the back of an animal
c. story

6. Paragraph 10 says:

"Casey was taking the mail to San Francisco."

Write the word that means *letters*.

7. Paragraph 13 says:

"The facts of the wreck don't seem to matter much now."

Write the word that means *crash*.

8. Paragraph 2 says:

"Ahead of him there was a slow freight train."

This time, write the word that means the <u>opposite</u> of *fast*.

Alphabetical Order. To put words in alphabetical, or a-b-c order, look at the first letters of the words. These words are in alphabetical order:

1. back	2. may	3. today
car	might	took
full	more	town

9. Which word would you put next after the word *nickname*?

a. engineer
b. freight
c. respect

10. Look again at the words in question 9. Which word would you put next after the word *forgotten*?

Thinking Skills BOOK 2 SELECTION 3

Identifying Similarities. In each question, choose the word that goes best in the blank space.

1. An ENGINEER drives a TRAIN, just as a PILOT drives a(n) _____.

    a. airplane
    b. bicycle
    c. car

2. "CASEY" was the nickname of the engineer JOHN LUTHER JONES, just as _____ was the nickname of the baseball player GEORGE HERMAN RUTH.

    a. "Babe"
    b. "George"
    c. "Herman"

Identifying Relationships. Look carefully at the pairs of words in capitals. Try to figure out the relationships between each pair. Then choose the sentence that does the <u>best</u> job of showing how the words are related.

3. CASEY JONES : SONG

    a. Casey Jones is the hero of a song.
    b. Casey Jones liked to sing songs.
    c. Casey Jones wrote a famous song.

4. CANNONBALL : CHALLENGER

    a. A cannonball is a challenger to enemy troops.
    b. The "Cannonball" ran into a freight train named "Challenger."
    c. The "Cannonball" was destroyed in an accident, just as the space shuttle "Challenger" was.

5. SEIBERT : JONES

    a. Seibert's last name was really Jones.
    b. Seibert was Jones's friend.
    c. Seibert wrote a song about Jones.

How do you put out a fire? You throw water on it, right? But there are times when throwing water on a fire is not a good idea at all.

4. Fires That Water Won't Put Out

1   Throw water on a fire in a wastebasket. What happens? It goes out.

2   Now pour water on a drum of burning oil. This time, does the fire go out? No. It keeps burning.

3   And try to pour water on an electrical fire! What happens? You guessed it. Nothing. That is, if you don't step in the water! If you do, something happens, all right. You may get electrocuted.

4   Why does water put out some fires and not others? It depends on the fire. Water puts out fire by cooling it off. If you throw water on paper, it can't burn. It can't stay hot enough.

5   But pour water on burning oil, and something else happens. Oil floats on water. So the water sinks under the oil. And the oil keeps on burning.

6   Many liquids that burn act like oil. That is, they float on water. So water is no good to put out this type of fire. Don't try to put out a gasoline fire with water. You may just spread it instead.

7   The same goes for a grease fire. If grease in a pan catches fire, forget about water. It won't help. Toss salt on it instead. The salt soaks up the grease. And the fire goes out.

GLOSSARY

electrical	With electricity. *Example:* Electrical wires carry electricity to all parts of the house.
electrocuted	Killed by an electric shock. *Example:* If you touch a bare electric wire, you can be electrocuted.
fire extinguisher	A piece of equipment used to put out fires. *Example:* Janet grabbed the fire extinguisher from the wall and began to spray the fire.
liquid	Something that is wet, like water. *Example:* The liquid flowed between his fingers.

8   What about electrical fires? These usually start from bad wiring. Maybe a wire is worn through. Water is dangerous here. Electricity flows through water just like it flows through a wire. You can get killed if you pour water on an electrical fire.

9   So how do you put out an oil fire or an electrical fire? You get a fire extinguisher. But you must get a special kind of extinguisher. The ordinary kind is no good. It sprays out water. You can't use it on burning oil. You can't use it on an electrical fire.

10   The special kinds of fire extinguisher don't use water. Some use a powder. Some use a gas. Both kinds put out a fire by cutting off the fire's air supply. A fire can't burn without air.

11   You need a special extinguisher in a car repair shop. It will put out gasoline and oil fires. You also need a special extinguisher in a welding shop. It will put out electrical fires. Be sure you get the right kind. Look at the label on the extinguisher. It tells you what kind of fire it should be used on.

12   Don't get caught by a fire that water won't put out!

Reading Skills

1. Which fire will water put out?

   a. electrical fire
   b. fire in a drum of oil
   c. fire in a wastebasket

2. What happens when water is poured on burning oil?

   a. the fire goes out
   b. the oil floats on the water
   c. the water catches fire

3. How do you put out an oil fire?

   a. blow on it
   b. pour water on it
   c. use a special fire extinguisher

4. (Paragraph 4) How does water put out a fire?

   a. cools it
   b. heats it
   c. steams it

5. (Paragraph 7) To put out a grease fire in a kitchen,

   a. use butter
   b. use salt
   c. use water

6. The story says that it you pour water on an electrical fire, you may get

   a. a bad shock
   b. a bright flame
   c. a medal from the fire department

7. What's in the special fire extinguishers?

   a. oil or electricity
   b. powder or gas
   c. water

8. How can you tell what kind of fire a fire extinguisher is good for?

   a. you can't tell
   b. you guess
   c. you read the label on the extinguisher

9. For an electrical fire, use a special fire extinguisher. What else do you think you should do?

   a. grasp hold of the wire
   b. pour water on the fire
   c. turn off the electricity

10. A gasoline fire acts most like

    a. an electrical fire
    b. an oil fire
    c. a paper fire

Vocabulary Skills BOOK 2
SELECTION 4

Glossary Check. Find the Glossary word that should go in each sentence. Then write the word.

1. When he touched the wire, the man was _____.

2. Milk is a _____.

Word Meanings. The meaning of a word depends on how the word is used.

3. Paragraph 2 says:
   "Now pour water on a drum of burning oil."

   In this sentence, what does *drum* mean?

   a. big can
   b. part of your ear
   c. something used in a band

4. Paragraph 6 says:
   "Many liquids that burn act like oil."

   In this sentence, what does *act* mean?

   a. behave
   b. pretend
   c. take part in a play

5. Paragraph 11 says:

   "You also need a special extinguisher in a welding shop."

   In this sentence, what does **shop** mean?

   a. buy
   b. place to work
   c. store

6. Paragraph 7 says:

   "Toss salt on it instead."

   Write the word that means **throw**.

7. Paragraph 8 says:

   "These usually start from bad wiring."

   Write the word that means **begin.**

8. Paragraph 8 says:

   "Maybe a wire is worn through. Water is dangerous here."

   This time, write the word that means the <u>opposite</u> of **safe**.

Using Apostrophes. The meaning of a word or a sentence may depend on how apostrophes are used.

9. Paragraph 4 says: "It can't stay hot enough."
   What is another way to write **It can't**?

   a. It can
   b. It cannot
   c. It was not

10. Paragraph 7 says: "It won't help."
    What is another way to write **won't help**?

    a. we do not help
    b. will help
    c. will not help

Thinking Skills BOOK 2 SELECTION 4

Things in Common. Looking at a list of things and seeing what they all have in common is a valuable thinking skill.

1. Look at the following list of words:

    oil   grease   gasoline

    The <u>best</u> and <u>most complete</u> way to describe these words to someone is to say that they are all

    a. kinds of water
    b. liquids that will burn
    c. wet things

2. Look at these words:

    fire   flood   earthquake   volcano

    Again, which of the following describes all the words <u>best</u> and <u>most completely</u>?

    a. things that burn
    b. things that destroy
    c. things that heal

Definitions. When you define a word, you often have to start off by thinking about what general kind of thing it is.

3. Look at the definition of the word *fire extinguisher* in the Glossary. It says a fire extinguisher is a piece of equipment.
   What is the best way to describe what general kind of thing a *chair* is?

    a. a machine
    b. an object
    c. a piece of furniture

4. What's the best way to describe what kind of thing a *waste basket* is?

    a. a container
    b. the round thing next to my desk
    c. when you don't want something anymore

5. A definition often starts out with telling something general. Then it goes on to give more information about the word.

    Look at the definition of *electrocuted* in the Glossary. Then look at this definition:

    strangled   Killed . . .

    This definition is incomplete. The best way to complete it would be to add the words

    a. by being squeezed around the neck
    b. in an upleasant way
    c. until you die

The story of Jed Smith, the trapper who explored the entire West before he was 30.

5. The Trapper Who Helped Win the West

1   You might say Jedediah Strong Smith had bad luck:

He spent part of his life looking for a river that did not exist.

He got rich. But he never had the chance to enjoy his money.

He was a great explorer. But until recently, he was all but unknown.

He died when he was only 32.

2   But you could look at it another way. Jed Smith led a wild, dangerous life. He had to have good luck just to get through each day alive!

3   Jed was born in New York State in 1799. As a boy, he read about the unknown West. And then when he was 23, he went west himself. At that time the land between the Rocky Mountains and California was known only to the Indians. Some said there were rivers full of beavers there. That's where Jed decided to go. He would explore the rivers and trap beavers. He could make money selling the beaver skins back in the East.

GLOSSARY

beaver   A small furry animal that often builds dams across streams.
Example: The woman wore a coat of beaver fur.

desert   A very dry part of the earth.
Example: Very little rain falls in the desert.

explorer   A person who looks for new lands.
Example: Columbus was an explorer who found America.

recently   Not too long ago.
Example: He has been away for a month, so I haven't seen him recently.

scalp   The skin on the top of the head.
Example: A branch of the tree fell on him and cut his scalp.

---

4   Jed found more than beavers in the West. He found deserts that took months to cross. He found Indians on the warpath. Once he found a bear. Jed came away with a torn ear, broken ribs, and a scalp cut to the bone. Somehow his luck held out and he lived. He got out of one scrape after another.

5   Jed kept pushing on. One of the things he was looking for was a river called the Buenaventura. The stories he had heard said that this river cut right through the mountains. Jed kept looking for it. He never found it, for it was not there. But he did get lots of beaver skins. And he blazed a trail through the West for others to follow.

6   Jed was the first American to:

- Walk from the Rocky Mountains to California.

- Cross the great deserts of Nevada.

- Cross the Sierra Nevada Mountains.

- Explore the whole West Coast.

- Make maps of the unknown West.

7   He did all that before he was 30. By then he was tired of adventure. He wanted to go back to a quiet place. He wanted to write a book. He wanted to spend the money he had made from trapping beavers.

8   But before he could finish his book, he took one more trip. He joined a wagon train headed for New Mexico. That was his last trip. His luck ran out. On the trail, the wagon train got lost. Jed went out, alone, to look for water. A group of Indians found him and killed him.

9   After his death, his books and maps were burned or got lost. He was almost forgotten. Men who came after him got more fame. But today, Jed Smith is remembered for what he was. He is remembered as a great explorer who helped win the West.

Reading Skills BOOK 2 SELECTION 5

1. Jed Smith is best known as

    a. an explorer
    b. a general
    c. a Senator

2. How did he help win the West?

    a. he fought against the Communists
    b. he found out a lot about the country west of the Rocky Mountains
    c. he was on one of the first boats to land in America

3. (Paragraph 4) The story tells about a time when he found a bear. What happened?

    a. the bear and Jed became friends
    b. the bear hurt Jed badly
    c. the bear ran away

4. (Paragraph 5) How long did it take Jed to find the Buenaventura River?

    a. he found it right away
    b. it took him several years, but he found it
    c. he never did find it

5. (Paragraph 8) How did Jed die?

    a. he shot himself
    b. his own men killed him
    c. Indians killed him

6. Where did he die?

    a. alone on the trail
    b. in a hospital
    c. in his own house

7. How much did Jed travel?

    a. about the same as most men of his time
    b. much more than most men of his time
    c. he stayed in one place most of his life

8. How long did he live?

    a. he died young
    b. he lived to a fairly old age
    c. he lived longer than any other man of his time

9. Where did Jed like to live most?

    a. in cities
    b. in wild country
    c. on farms

10. Which of these men was most like Jed?

    a. Babe Ruth
    b. Daniel Boone
    c. John D. Rockefeller

Vocabulary Skills BOOK 2 SELECTION 5

Glossary Check. Find the Glossary word that should go in each sentence. Then write the word.

1. Your hair grows out of your _____.

2. The first man to go to the North Pole was a great _____.

Word Meanings. The meaning of a word depends on how the word is used.

3. Paragraph 1 says:
   "He spent part of his life looking for a river that did not exist."

   In this sentence, what does **spent** mean?

   a. paid money
   b. passed
   c. tired out

4. Paragraph 2 says:

   "Jed Smith led a wild, dangerous life."

   In this sentence, what does *led* mean?

   a. a kind of metal
   b. at the head of
   c. went through

5. Paragraph 3 says:

   "He could make money selling the beaver skins back in the East."

   In this sentence, what does *back* mean?

   a. at home
   b. in the past
   c. part of the body

6. Paragraph 5 says:

   "The stories he had heard said that this river cut right through the mountains."

   Write the word that means *tales*.

7. Paragraph 4 says:

   ". . . the money he had made from trapping beavers."

   Write the word that means *catching*.

8. Paragraph 4 says:

   "Somehow his luck held out and he lived."

   This time, write the word that means the <u>opposite</u> of *died*.

Prefixes. The prefix *un-* often means "not . . ."

Paragraph 3 says: ". . . he read about the unknown West."

9. What does *unafraid* mean?

   a. afraid
   b. not afraid
   c. not brave

10. What does *unhappy* mean?

    a. happy
    b. not healthy
    c. sad

Thinking Skills BOOK 2 SELECTION 5

Correct Order. Putting things in correct order is an important thinking skill.

1. Look at the list below. Put the items in order of <u>time</u>, from first to last.
   (1 = first, 2 = second, 3 = last)

   a. ___ Jed joined a wagon train headed for New Mexico.
   b. ___ Jed moved from New York State.
   c. ___ Jed started writing a book.

2. Look at the list. Put the items in order of <u>space</u>, from east to west.
   (1 = farthest east, 2 = farther west, 3 = farthest west)

   a. ___ California
   b. ___ New York State
   c. ___ Rocky Mountains

3. Look at the list of Jed Smith's achievements. Put the items in order of <u>importance</u> to us today, from most important to least important.
   (1 = most, 2 = less, 3 = least)

   a. ___ Jed explored the entire West Coast.
   b. ___ Jed fought a bear.
   c. ___ Jed showed that the Buenaventura didn't exist.

Cause and Effect. Look at these two sentences:

   Billie told a joke. Everybody laughed.

Telling a joke caused everybody to laugh. The telling is the ***cause***. Everybody laughing is the ***effect***. We say that the two sentences show a ***cause-effect*** relationship.

4. Check the pair of sentences below that have a cause-effect relationship in the story. (The first is the reason for the second, or causes the second.)

   a. Jed fought a bear. He lost part of his scalp.
   b. Jed made maps of the West. Later, they were lost.
   c. Jed walked across the Rockies. He trapped beavers there.

5. Again, check the pair that have a cause-effect relationship.

   a. Jed looked for the Buenaventura River. He never found it.
   b. Jed started writing a book. He took one more trip before he finished it.
   c. Jed was tired of adventure. He decided to settle down.

A giant stone man was the main character in one of the most famous hoaxes of all time.

6. A Giant Hoax

1   It was a cold day in 1889. On a farm near the town of Cardiff in New York State, two men were digging a well. They worked for a farmer named Newell. Five feet down, they hit a huge rock. They worked hard to dig it out of the soil. When the rock was free, they found that it was not a rock at all. It looked like a man. They brushed off the dirt. It was a man. He was about 12 feet (nearly 4 meters) tall! The men thought they had found a fossil.

2   Newell, who owned the farm, thought so too. He called a friend at the newspaper. Reporters from the paper came to see the find. They called it the "Cardiff Giant." Soon all the world knew of the strange find. But it was hard to believe in a man that tall!

3   Soon scientists came to the farm. They all wanted to see the Giant. They walked around him. They looked at him. They tapped him. They drew pictures of him. Some said that the Giant was a true fossil. They said that he had been a real man at one time. Others said that the Giant was a statue. They said he was very old. They said he had been carved by some ancient tribe. A few scientists said that it was all a joke. One said that the figure was made of gypsum. He said it had not been in the ground for long.

4   Newell did not care what the Giant was. He did not care if it was a joke. Everyone wanted to see his Giant, and Newell knew that they would pay to see him. Newell built a tent over his discovery. Soon people were lined up to see the Giant. They paid $1.00 to see him. And in those days $1.00 was a lot of cash.

GLOSSARY

fossil	The remains of an ancient living thing *Example:* The museum has dinosaur fossils.
furious	Very angry. *Example:* Roger was furious when I beat him at checkers.
gypsum	A mineral sometimes used to make plaster. *Example:* Gypsum is soft enough to carve with a knife.
hoax	Something that pretends to be real; a joke; a prank. *Example:* Do you think the story about flying saucers is a hoax?

5   The great showman P. T. Barnum also heard about the Cardiff Giant. Barnum ran a circus. He tried to buy the Giant for his circus, but Newell would not sell. So Barnum paid a stonecutter to carve a statue that looked just like the Giant in Newell's field. Barnum put the fake Cardiff Giant in his circus. People lined up to see Barnum's fake.

6   Newell heard what Barnum was doing. He was furious. He said people would not come to see his Giant. He said they would go to see the fake one. At the circus they could see the Giant and many other strange things too. So Newell went to court. He asked the judge to stop Barnum. Barnum said that both Giants were fakes. He said that there was nothing wrong in showing a fake of a fake. The judge thought Barnum was right.

7   While all this was happening, a reporter was looking for the truth. He learned that Newell's cousin, George Hull, had bought a huge block of gypsum. Hull had hired a stonecutter. He had sent a large crate to a town near Newell's farm. Hull *said* that the crate held a machine. It all began to make sense. The reporter felt sure the crate had held the stone man.

8   Hull told the truth. He said that it was all a joke. He told what he did to fool people. He had someone carve the man. They rubbed it with ink to make it look dirty. They poured acid on it so that it looked worn. They poked holes in it. Then they buried it. After 2 years the stone man looked as if he had been in the ground a long time.

9   Hull said that the joke had cost him $2,200. But Newell had made $35,000 from the hoax. In the towns of New York State, people still tell and retell the story of the Cardiff Giant.

Reading Skills BOOK 2
SELECTION 6

1. The giant hoax was a

   a. statue in the ground
   b. strong man
   c. wild animal

2. The Cardiff Giant was found by

   a. men digging a well
   b. P. T. Barnum
   c. a scientist

3. Why did people want to see the Giant?

   a. He was pretty
   b. He was strange
   c. He was dirty

4. (Paragraph 3) The scientists

   a. all thought it was a fossil
   b. all thought it was a statue
   c. could not agree

5. (Paragraph 4) Newell charged people money to

   a. dig for statues
   b. see the stone man
   c. see the scientists

6. (Paragraph 5) P. T. Barnum wanted to buy the Giant

   a. to sell again
   b. to give to a museum
   c. to put in his circus

7. The judge said that Barnum

   a. could show his own Giant
   b. must stop showing giants
   c. must pay Newell for the Giant

8. Hull put acid on the statue to make it

    a. bigger
    b. look worn
    c. disappear

9. Newell went to court to sue

    a. Barnum
    b. Cardiff
    c. Hull

10. Who made the most money from the hoax?

    a. Hull
    b. Newell
    c. a reporter

Vocabulary Skills BOOK 2 SELECTION 6

Glossary Check. Find the Glossary word that should go in each sentence.
    Then write the word.

1. The story about cows playing baseball was a _____.

2. The science teacher has a display of _fossil_ sea shells in the lab.

Word Meanings. The meaning of a word depends on how the word is used.

3. Paragraph 5 says:
    "Barnum ran a circus."

    In this sentence, what does *ran* mean?

    a. moved fast
    b. operated
    c. worked in

4. Paragraph 3 says:
    "He said it had not been in the ground for long."

    In this sentence, what does *long* mean?

    a. a lot of time
    b. tall
    c. want badly

5. Paragraph 3 says:

   "They tapped him."

   In this sentence, what does **tapped** mean?

   a. chose
   b. struck lightly
   c. recorded on tape

6. Paragraph 5 says:

   "One day P. T. Barnum heard about the strange man."

   Write the word that means **odd**.

7. Paragraph 6 says:

   "He said they would go to see the fake one."

   Write the word that means **not real**.

8. Paragraph 2 says:

   "He called a friend at the newspaper."

   This time, write the word that means the <u>opposite</u> of **enemy.**

Prefixes. The prefix **re-** often means "again" or "back."

Paragraph 9 says: "People still tell and retell this story in the towns of New York State."

The word **retell** means "tell again."

The word **repay** means "pay back what you owe."

9. What does **remake** mean?

   a. do for the first time
   b. make over again
   c. take away

10. What does **replace** mean?

   a. find a place
   b. pick up
   c. put back again

Thinking Skills BOOK 2 SELECTION 6

Things in Common. Looking at a list of things and seeing what they all have in common is a valuable thinking skill.

1. Look at the following list of words:

   Newell   P.T. Barnum   Hull

   The best and most complete way to describe these words to someone is to say that they are all

   a. farmers
   b. hoaxers
   c. people

2. Look at these words:

   fossil   statue   mountains   buildings

   Again, which of the following describes all the words best and most completely?

   a. things often used for hoaxes
   b. things that look like living creatures
   c. things often made of stone

Definitions. When you define a word, you often have to start off by thinking about what general kind of thing it is.

3. Look at the definition of the word *gypsum* in the Glossary. It says gypsum is a mineral.
   What is the best way to describe what general kind of thing *lettuce* is?

   a. green
   b. a head
   c. a vegetable

4. What is the best way to describe what kind of thing a *reporter* is?

   a. they report
   b. a writer
   c. you can't always believe them

5. A definition often starts out with telling something general. Then it goes on to give more information about the word.

   Look at the definition of *fossil* in the Glossary. Then look at this definition:

   footprint   A mark on the ground . . .

   This definition is incomplete. The best way to complete it would be to add the words

   a. a foot long
   b. made by a foot
   c. that was printed in the ground

The story of what happened to a group of settlers trapped in the driest and hottest desert in the United States.

7. How Death Valley Got Its Name

1   In the 1800's many Americans were moving West. There are many tales that tell of those trips. This is one of them.

2   In October, 1849, hundreds of people met near Salt Lake City in Utah. They had everything they owned with them. They hoped to find a new life in California.

3   They knew that the trip would be rough. There were miles and miles of desert to cross.

4   They started out together. A guide went with them. But there was no trail. There were no more than a few water holes, and there was nothing to see but small dry plants, dry grass, and mountains.

5   On Christmas Eve, 1849, a strange sight met their eyes. They had come to one of the loneliest spots in the world. It was a deep valley that lay 282 feet below sea level. It was drier, hotter, and lonelier than anything they had seen before.

6   The wagons started through the valley. The pioneers were all low on food. They found water—lakes of it. But it was salt water. It wasn't fit to drink.

7   It was too late to turn back. They had gone too far. Yet many were too weak to go on. Someone had to go ahead and find food. Two of the strongest men were picked as scouts. With little food and water, the scouts set out on foot.

8   Their food and water were soon gone. Still they kept on. Their thirst grew worse and worse.

GLOSSARY

Death Valley	A large, hot, dry valley in California. *Example:* There are high mountains all around Death Valley.
desert	A dry area where rain hardly ever falls. *Example:* It is hard to find water in the desert.
graveyard	A place where people are buried. *Example:* There are hundreds of dead men in the graveyard.
pioneers	The first people to move to new parts of the country. *Example:* Long ago, pioneers left the East and moved to the West.

---

9   Finally they got out of the valley. But there was still more desert in front of them. The sun burned them by day. At night the air was ice cold. In one spot they found a thin sheet of ice. They broke off little pieces, and for a while they had water to drink.

10   At last they came to a town. They had reached the rich San Fernando Valley near Los Angeles.

11   The scouts stocked up with food and water. Then they turned back to the desert. Their friends had almost given up all hope. The scouts had been gone for four weeks.

12   The scouts told the pioneers of the hard trip ahead. The women dressed themselves and their children in their best clothes. The men strapped two water bags to the back of an ox. Then they set off.

13   Only 15 people lived to walk out of the valley. They had lost everything they owned. The valley was the graveyard of their families, their friends, and their hopes.

14   As they left, they turned to look back one last time. The men took off their hats. They stood for a moment. Then one man said, "Good-by, Death Valley."

15   And so Death Valley was named.

Reading Skills BOOK 2
SELECTION 7

1. How did Death Valley get its name?

   a. anybody who goes there, dies
   b. a group of pioneers died there
   c. it is a valley in the Death Mountains

2. Death Valley is in

   a. the desert
   b. the middle of a forest
   c. the ocean

3. What happened to the pioneers in Death Valley?

   a. Indians killed most of them
   b. most of them died because they had nothing to eat or drink
   c. most of them finally got out, tired but safe

4. (Paragraph 2) The pioneers started out from

   a. California
   b. Death Valley
   c. Utah

5. (Paragraph 6) A man who looks for water in Death Valley will find

   a. lots of good drinking water
   b. no water at all
   c. some water, but none fit to drink

6. (Paragraph 9) What was the desert like on the other side of Death Valley?

   a. cold all the time
   b. hot all the time
   c. hot in the day, but cold at night

7. How long were the scouts gone from Death Valley?

   a. about a week
   b. about a month
   c. about a year

8. Death Valley is

    a. above sea level
    b. at sea level
    c. below sea level

9. When the men left Death Valley, they took off their hats and stood for a while. Why do you think they did this?

    a. to cool off their heads
    b. to feel the warmth of the sun
    c. to pay respect to their dead friends

10. Why didn't the people who were stuck in Death Valley turn around and go back?

    a. they had come too far and were too weak
    b. they thought they would like to live there
    c. they were afraid of Indians

Vocabulary Skills BOOK 2 SELECTION 7

Glossary Check. Find the Glossary word that should go in each sentence. Then write the word.

1. California was settled by _____.

2. Death Valley is a _____, so we know that it doesn't have very much water.

Word Meanings. The meaning of a word depends on how the word is used.

3. Paragraph 3 says:
"They knew that the trip would be rough."

In this sentence, what does **rough** mean?

    a. full of waves
    b. not sure
    c. very hard

4. Paragraph 4 says:
"But there was no trail."

In this sentence, what does **trail** mean?

    a. follow
    b. marks left by an animal
    c. road or path

5. Paragraph 9 says:

"In one spot they found a thin sheet of ice."

In this sentence, what does **sheet** mean?

a. cloth for a bed
b. flat piece
c. page of paper

6. Paragraph 1 says:

"There are many tales that tell of those trips."

Write the word that means **stories**.

7. Paragraph 11 says:

"The scouts stocked up with food and water."

Write the word that means **loaded**.

8. Paragraph 2 says:

"They had everything they owned with them."

This time, write the word that means the <u>opposite</u> of **nothing**.

Suffixes. The suffix **-est** often means "the most..."

Paragraph 5 says: "They had come to one of the loneliest spots in the world."

The word **loneliest** means "most lonely."

The word **biggest** means "most big."

9. What does **hardest** mean?

a. hardly
b. most hard
c. most lard

10. What does **longest** mean?

a. longer
b. most long
c. most wrong

Thinking Skills BOOK 2
SELECTION 7

Identifying Similarities. In each question, choose the word that goes best in the blank space.

    1. A HORSE moves a WAGON, just as
       an ENGINE moves a _____.

       a. car
       b. drill
       c. saw

    2. A DESERT is a place that is DRY, just as
       a _____ is a place that is WET.

       a. hill
       b. mountain
       c. swamp

Identifying Relationships. Look carefully at the pairs of words in capitals. Try to figure out the relationships between each pair. Then choose the sentence that does the <u>best</u> job of showing how the words are related.

    3. WATER : THIRST

       a. Before you drink water you are always thirsty.
       b. Lack of water causes thirst.
       c. Water makes you thirsty.

    4. HEAT : COLD

       a. Heat is the opposite of cold.
       b. If something isn't hot, it must be cold.
       c. Heat comes before cold.

    5. GRASS : PLANT

       a. Grass and plants are green.
       b. Grass and plants both grow in the ground.
       c. Grass is a kind of plant.

The continents of the earth look as if they fit together like a giant jigsaw puzzle. Do you know the reason?

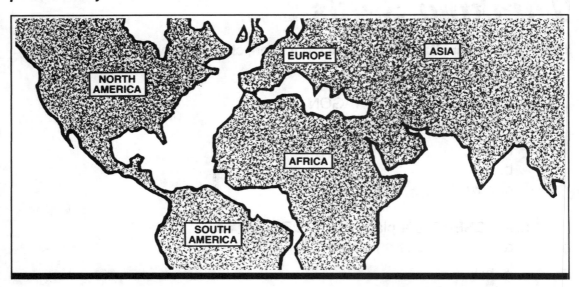

8. The Floating Continents

1   What is about 4 thousand miles long and moves a half-inch a year? Would you believe North America? And South America too? And Europe and Africa?

2   The answer is a strange one. It's even stranger than the question. North America is a continent. They're all continents. And everyone knows continents can't move. They're part of the earth itself. Right?

3   But more than 50 years ago a scientist named Alfred Wegener looked at a map of the world. He noticed that it looked like a jigsaw puzzle. The coast of North and South America looked like one big piece. The coast of Europe and Africa looked like another piece. The coasts looked as if they would fit together.

4   Wegener decided that long ago the continents really did fit together. Then something happened, and they drifted apart.

5   Everyone laughed at poor Wegener. How could continents drift? And if they moved, what pushed them?

6   So Wegener's idea died. But new facts about earth kept turning up. Among the facts were:

★ Fossils of animals were found near the South Pole. But these animals could only have lived in hot places.

GLOSSARY

continent	A huge piece of land, bigger than an island. *Example:* There are 13 countries on the continent of South America.
drift	To move slowly and without purpose. *Example:* The boat drifted slowly down the stream.
fossils	Bones of animals that died millions of years ago. *Example:* Dinosaur bones are all fossils.
jigsaw puzzle	A puzzle you put together from lots of little pieces. *Example:* When we put the jigsaw puzzle together, we had a picture of an Indian.
ripped	Torn. *Example:* June's jacket was ripped.

★ Rocks in South America were a match for rocks in Africa. The rocks matched only where the two continents would touch in a jigsaw puzzle fit.

★ Computers studied the problem and they showed that the jigsaw puzzle fit was even better than Wegener thought.

7   There is only one way to explain these facts. Wegener was right. The continents do move. Today we know something about how they do it.

8   The crust of earth is made up of a few huge jigsaw-puzzle pieces of rock. These pieces are called "plates." The oceans rest on top of the plates. The plates form the ocean bottom. The land part of the continents rests on the plates too.

9   Under the plates, the earth is made of melted rock. The plates float on this liquid rock. They can move around, like rafts on a pond. And so the continents, which are held up by the plates, move too.

10   Some continents sit on two plates at once. If the plates moved apart, the continent would be ripped in two. Part would stay on one plate. Part would stay on the other. And, on a map, the two halves would match, just like a jigsaw puzzle.

11   Long ago this is what happened to America, Europe, and Africa. They used to be a single super-continent. But this super-continent was sitting on two plates. The plates moved apart. The super-continent split in two. America traveled west. Europe and Africa traveled east. Water filled the space between them. This water is the Atlantic Ocean.

12   The continents are still moving apart today. Maybe some day they will bump into each other again on the other side of the world!

Reading Skills BOOK 2 SELECTION 8

1. This selection tells about continents that are

   a. moving apart
   b. floating in one place without moving
   c. turning around in circles

2. The continents sit on top of

   a. oceans
   b. other continents
   c. plates

3. The plates float on top of

   a. continents
   b. liquid rock
   c. oceans

4. (Paragraph 3) Wegener got his ideas from

   a. books about lost continents
   b. floating around on continents during his vacation
   c. looking at a world map

5. (Paragraph 5) What did other scientists think about Wegener?

   a. they didn't believe him
   b. they gave him prizes for his idea
   c. they never heard of him

6. (Paragraph 9) Why do continents move?

   a. they are pushed by ocean waves
   b. they are pushed by other continents
   c. they sit on moving plates

7. Let's say a continent is resting on two plates. If the plates move apart, what happens to the continent?

   a. it is torn apart
   b. it goes off on one of the plates, but not on the other
   c. it sinks into the ocean

8. When continents move apart, what fills the space between them?

  a. air
  b. nothing
  c. ocean

9. What part of America do you think once touched Africa?

  a. Alaska, in northern North America
  b. California, in the western U.S.A.
  c. Brazil, in eastern South America

10. The continents move apart less than an inch a year. This means that the time they were together was

  a. about 50 years ago
  b. less than a thousand years ago
  c. millions and millions of years ago

Vocabulary Skills BOOK 2 SELECTION 8

Glossary Check. Find the Glossary word that should go in each sentence. Then write the word.

  1. Asia is the largest _____.

  2. The bones of cave people are all _____.

Word Meanings. The meaning of a word depends on how the word is used.

  3. Paragraph 6 says:
  "But new facts about earth kept turning up."

  In this sentence, what does **turning up** mean?

  a. being discovered
  b. moving right side up
  c. spinning upward

  4. Paragraph 6 says:
  "Rocks in South America were a match for rocks in Africa."

  In this sentence, what does **match** mean?

  a. athletic contest
  b. fit
  c. something you light fires with

5. Paragraph 8 says:

"The oceans rest on top of the plates."

In this sentence, what does **plates** mean?

a. dishes
b. pieces of the earth's crust
c. puts a coating of silver on something

6. Paragraph 5 says:

"His ideas seemed crazy."

Write the word that means **insane**.

7. Paragraph 7 says:

"Wegener was right."

Write the word that means **correct**.

8. Paragraph 9 says:

"The plates float on this liquid rock."

This time, write the word that means the <u>opposite</u> of **solid**.

Suffixes. The suffix **-er** often means "more . . ."

Paragraph 2 says: "It's even stranger than the question."

The word **stranger** means "more strange."

9. What does **bigger** mean?

a. biggest
b. larger in size
c. dig more

10. What does **easier** mean?

a. easiest
b. less easy
c. not as hard

Thinking Skills BOOK 2
SELECTION 8

Fact and Opinion. In your thinking, you should be able to tell a fact from an opinion.

"The sun is a star" is a **fact**. It can be proved by a scientist.
"George Washington was a great president" is an **opinion**. It may be a good opinion, but it's not something a scientist can prove.

1. Which of these statements states a **fact**? (choose one)

    a. Earth's crust is made of "plates."
    b. Scientists should listen to people like Wegner more carefully.
    c. Wegener was one of the finest scientists of this century.

2. Which of these statements states an **opinion**? (choose one)

    a. Rocks in South America match rocks in Africa.
    b. Scientists should have figured out long ago that continents float.
    c. Wegener decided that the continents once fit together.

Logical Thinking. Thinking logically means taking information and drawing the right conclusions from it.

3. Look at these statements:

    Land reptiles live only in warm climates.
    A land reptile fossil was found near the South Pole.

    Which conclusion is correct?

    a. Land reptiles live at the South Pole.
    b. The South Pole once had a warm climate.
    c. The South Pole is warm today.

4. Look at these statements:

    Jigsaw puzzles are made of pieces that fit together.
    Continents look something like jigsaw puzzle pieces.

    Which conclusion is correct? (Be careful on this one!)

    a. Continents are a puzzle.
    b. Continents definitely fit together.
    c. Continents look as if they fit together.

5. Look at these statements:

    Plates move.
    The ocean bottom is made of plates.

    Which conclusion is correct?

    a. The bottom of the ocean moves.
    b. The ocean is made of plates
    c. The ocean will cover the continents.

The ordinary jobs that seem safe—but that may be the most dangerous of all.

9. The Most Dangerous Jobs

1   What jobs do you think are the most dangerous? Diving for pearls? Working with dynamite? Building skyscrapers? Flying in a space shuttle? Those are a few of them. But some of the most dangerous jobs will come as a surprise to you. How about the job of baker? Or printer? Or painter? Surprisingly, these jobs are dangerous, too.

2   There are two types of dangers in jobs. The first is from accidents. The second is from sickness.

3   The first type is usually easy to tell. Someone who builds skyscrapers may fall. A space rocket can blow up. Divers who go deep down in the sea will die if they come up too fast.

4   The second type is harder to tell. Why should a baker's job be dangerous? The reason is that a baker works with flour. He or she needs it to make bread, rolls, and cakes. The flour dust gets into the lungs. That doesn't matter. Not for a few weeks, that is. But after months and years, lungs may get clogged. What happens next? TB! Or some other chest disease. This won't happen to all bakers. But it happens to some.

5   In a coal miner's job there's danger from both accidents and sickness. A miner can get killed if the mine caves in, or if there's a gas explosion.

GLOSSARY

lead	A kind of heavy metal. *Example:* The old water pipes were made of lead.
life insurance	A plan that costs you a little money each month and promises to pay your family a large sum of money if you die. *Example:* When Dr. Noguchi died, the life insurance paid over $100,000 to the Noguchi family.
skyscraper	A very tall building. *Example:* The Empire State Building in New York City is a skyscraper.
space rocket	A space ship. *Example:* The space rocket headed for the moon.
TB	Tuberculosis—a sickness of the lungs. *Example:* A person who has TB coughs a lot.

---

6   But he can also get sick. He digs with machines and shovels. A lot of dust gets kicked up. He breathes that dust. He breathes it for hours each day. After a while, he may get a chest disease.

7   What is there in a printer's job that might be harmful? Well, you may think of the huge machines in a print shop. That's not the main danger. It's the ink. The ink the printer uses may be poisonous. It may soak into the skin. It may get under the nails. Of course, the printer may never get sick from the ink. But if enough of it soaks into the body, it can cause death.

8   How about the painter's job? The danger isn't mainly from falling off ladders. The danger is the paint. Paint is like printer's ink. It can be poison. The job of a painter used to be even more dangerous. Some paints used to have lead in them. Lead is a very powerful poison. And if a person takes in too much lead, death can result.

9   How can you find out if your job is dangerous? See how hard it is to get life insurance. Is it easy for you to get cheap insurance? Then your job is fairly safe. But if it's hard for you to get life insurance, ask why. You may have one of the most dangerous jobs.

Reading Skills BOOK 2
SELECTION 9

1. This story tells you that

    a. all jobs are very dangerous
    b. some jobs that seem safe are really dangerous
    c. there are no dangerous jobs

2. There are two main types of dangers in jobs. The first is from accidents. The second is from

    a. mean bosses
    b. other workers
    c. sickness

3. (Paragraph 1) A dangerous job that might surprise you is that of

    a. baby-sitter
    b. baker
    c. writer

4. (Paragraph 4) TB is a

    a. baker
    b. disease
    c. flour

5. (Paragraph 7) The main danger in a printer's job is

    a. big machines
    b. dust
    c. ink

6. How does a printer get harmed by ink?

    a. by drinking it
    b. by being hit by it
    c. it soaks into the skin

7. At one time, the biggest danger to a painter was

    a. climbing ladders
    b. lead poisoning
    c. working too hard

8. How does the story say you can find out if your job is dangerous?

    a. ask your boss
    b. see how hard it is to get life insurance
    c. you can't find out

9. Sue Ellen Smith works where there is lots of dust in the air. Sue Ellen is in danger of getting

    a. a chest disease
    b. a leg disease
    c. a raise

10. Life insurance is very cheap for you. Your job is probably

    a. dangerous
    b. safe
    c. working in a coal mine

Vocabulary Skills BOOK 2 SELECTION 9

Glossary Check. Find the Glossary word that should go in each sentence. Then write the word.

1. Many people have died of _____.

2. There were 100 floors in the _____.

Word Meanings. The meaning of a word depends on how the word is used.

3. Paragraph 4 says:
   "That doesn't matter."

   In this sentence, what does *matter* mean?

   a. kind of material
   b. make a difference
   c. thing

4. Paragraph 8 says:
   "Lead is a poison."

   In this sentence, what does *lead* mean?

   a. go first
   b. kind of metal
   c. the first

5. Paragraph 9 says:

"Then your job is fairly safe."

In this sentence, what does **safe** mean?

   a. not dangerous
   b. on base
   c. place to keep your money

6. Paragraph 4 says:

"But after months and years, lungs may get clogged."

Write the word that means **filled up**.

7. Paragraph 7 says:

"Well, you may think of the huge machines in a print shop."

Write the word that means **big**.

8. Paragraph 6 says:

"But he can also get sick. He digs with machines and shovels."

This time, write the word that means the <u>opposite</u> of **well**.

Suffixes. The suffix **-ness** often means "being..." or "way of being...

Paragraph 2 says: "The second is from sickness."

The word **sickness** means "being sick."

The word **goodness** means "being good."

9. What does **happiness** mean?

   a. a happy man
   b. more happy
   c. way of being happy

10. What does **illness** mean?

   a. more ill
   b. most ill
   c. sickness

Thinking Skills BOOK 2 SELECTION 9

Identifying Similarities. In each question, choose the word that goes best in the blank space.

1. PAINTERS use PAINT, just as
PRINTERS use _____.

    a. ink
    b. presses
    c. machinery

2. BAKERS may breathe _____ into their lungs, just as
MINERS may breathe in DUST.

    a. bread
    b. cakes
    c. flour

Identifying Relationships. Look carefully at the pairs of words in capitals. Try to figure out the relationships between each pair. Then choose the sentence that does the best job of showing how the words are related.

3. COAL : MINE

    a. Coal comes from a mine.
    b. Coal is a kind of mine.
    c. Coal is mine if I have a stove.

4. DIVER : SEA

    a. Divers dive in the sea.
    b. Divers are helped by the sea.
    c. The sea is the opposite of a diver.

5. LUNGS : CHEST

    a. The chest is inside the lungs.
    b. The lungs are inside the chest.
    c. The lungs can make the chest sick.

The wonderful car that's owned by millionaires, princes, presidents—and a garbage collector.

10. *The Rolls-Royce*

1   How often do you and your family buy a car? Every year? Every 5 years? Most cars start to have things go wrong when they are about 3 years old. The motor starts to fail. The car may need new brakes. It may get rusty. As cars get older, they get worse.

2   There is an answer to this problem. Buy a Rolls-Royce. But check your bank book first. A Rolls-Royce will cost you between $100,000 and $200,000!

3   If you need to save up, you will have plenty of time. All Rolls-Royces are custom made. You tell the factory what you want. A team of workers builds your special car. It may take a year from the time you put in your order. Do you think you can save up enough money in a year?

4   What makes people willing to spend that much money for a car? Well, a Rolls-Royce is a special car.

5   The car was first built by Frederick Henry Royce. He was an English engineer. He bought his first car in 1883. It was noisy and it was always breaking down. He kept fixing the car and making it better. By 1904 Royce had built a car that was very quiet and never broke down.

6   In 1904 Royce met Charles Rolls. Rolls was very rich and raced cars as a hobby. He loved the Royce car. Rolls and Royce decided to go into business together. They wanted to build and sell cars. They gave the car they built their own names.

GLOSSARY

custom-made
Made to order.
Example: My cousins are so rich they have custom-made skate boards.

invest
To put money into.
Example: It pays to invest in good tires.

proceed
To move forward.
Example: When the light changes to green, you may proceed.

sheik
An Arab chief or ruler.
Example: The sheik's oil wells made him rich.

team
A group that works together.
Example: To play good basketball, you need a good team.

---

7   The cars got better and better. They never seemed to break down or wear out. In 1920 someone gave the Rolls-Royce factory an "old" Rolls-Royce car. It was a 1905 model. It had gone 100,000 miles (160,000 kilometers). It was still in perfect condition. One 1922 Rolls-Royce, still used, has gone more than 700,000 miles.

8   What makes a Rolls-Royce so special? Well, they are built very carefully. It takes 3 months to make one. Many parts are made by hand. The seats are made of the best leather. It takes 14 skins to make the seats in one car. Every car gets 14 coats of paint. Thin stripes around windows and doors are painted by hand. A mile of electric wiring goes into the car.

9   You can order special things. There are Rolls-Royces that have TV's. Some have built-in picnic baskets. Some have bars. Some even have fur rugs. But there is a limit. One Indian prince wanted to have some changes made in his six Rolls-Royces. They company refused. Furious, the prince had all six turned into garbage trucks.

10   A Rolls-Royce is made to last a lifetime. If you invest in one you may never have to buy another car. And you will be in good company. Kings and queens have them. So do Arab sheiks. And presidents. One Indian religious leader had more than 90.

11   And if you think owning your own Rolls-Royce is only a dream, think of Colin Phillips. When he was 16, Colin set his heart on owning one. In 1984, after collecting garbage six days a week for five years, he bought one. "It was hard work," he said, "but rubbish is all I know."

Reading Skills BOOK 2
SELECTION 10

1. This story is about a

   a. man
   b. car
   c. factory

2. A Rolls-Royce is

   a. very small
   b. very expensive
   c. able to run without gas

3. (Paragraph 6) The first Rolls-Royce was built in

   a. 1883
   b. 1920
   c. 1904

4. (Paragraph 6) Charles Rolls was a(n)

   a. engineer
   b. racing car driver
   c. Arab sheik

5. (Paragraph 8) A Rolls-Royce

   a. gets 14 coats of paint
   b. gets three coats of paint
   c. is sprayed by machine

6. How long will a Rolls-Royce last?

   a. about 10 years
   b. about 100,000 miles (160,000 kilometers)
   c. a lifetime

7. How much will a Rolls-Royce cost?

   a. between $10,000 and $20,000
   b. between $100,000 and $200,000
   c. two million dollars

8. What was unusual about Colin Phillips buying a Rolls-Royce?

   a. he already had 90 of them
   b. he earned the money collecting trash
   c. he wanted to turn it into a garbage truck

9. The Rolls-Royce is made in

   a. America
   b. Canada
   c. England

10. How often would you expect to find a Rolls-Royce in a junkyard?

   a. often
   b. never
   c. once in a while

Vocabulary Skills BOOK 2 SELECTION 10

Glossary Check. Find the Glossary word that should go in each sentence. Then write the word.

1. My feet are so big I need to wear _____ shoes.

2. I _____ every spare cent I have in my stamp collection.

Word meanings. The meaning of a word depends on how the word is used.

3. Paragraph 2 says:
   "But check your bank book first."

   In this sentence, what does **check** mean?
   a. money
   b. look at
   c. make a mark

4. Paragraph 7 says:
   "It was a 1905 model."

   In this sentence, what does **model** mean?
   a. a beautiful woman
   b. style
   c. toy car

5. Paragraph 10 says:
   "And you will be in good company."

   In this sentence, what does **company** mean?
   a. a group
   b. an army unit
   c. a business

6. Paragraph 9 says:
   "Furious, the prince had all six turned into garbage trucks."

   Write the word that means **angry**.

7. Paragraph 11 says:
   "It was hard work, but rubbish is all I know."

   Write the word that means **trash**.

8. Paragraph 8 says:
   'Well, they are built very carefully."

   This time, write the word that means the <u>opposite</u> of **carelessly**.

Suffixes: The suffix **-er** often means **more**.
The word **bigger** means **more big.**
The word **sooner** means **more soon**, or **earlier**.

9. What does **quieter** mean?

   a. always quiet
   b. more quiet
   c. never quiet

10. What does **older** mean?

   a. more old
   b. less old
   c. young

Thinking Skills BOOK 2 SELECTION 10

Fact and Opinion. In your thinking, you should be able to tell a fact from an opinion.

"The sun is a star" is a **fact**. It can be proved by a scientist.
"George Washington was a great president" is an **opinion**. It may be a good opinion, but it's not something a scientist can prove.

1. Which of these statements states a *fact*? (choose one)

    a. Frederick Royce built the first Rolls-Royce.
    b. No car is worth paying $200,000 for.
    c. The Rolls-Royce is worth what you pay for it.

2. Which of these statements states an *opinion*? (choose one)

    a. A mile of electric wiring goes into a Rolls-Royce.
    b. No one has ever built a better car than a Rolls-Royce.
    c. Rolls-Royces are made to last a lifetime.

Logical Thinking. Thinking logically means taking information and drawing the right conclusions from it.

3. Look at these statements:

    All fine cars are made of good materials.
    A Rolls-Royce is a fine car.

    Which conclusion is correct?

    a. All fine cars are made of the same materials as the Rolls-Royce.
    b. A Rolls-Royce is made of good materials.
    c. Only Rolls-Royce uses good materials.

4. Look at these statements:

    A Rolls-Royce takes a year to build and costs more than $90,000.
    Jenny Soto earns $30,000 a year.

    Which conclusion is correct?

    a. Jenny will never be able to afford a Rolls-Royce.
    b. Jenny cannot save enough money to buy a Rolls-Royce while it is being built.
    c. Jenny will not buy a Rolls-Royce.

5. Look at these statements:

    Someone who can easily afford a Rolls-Royce is not poor.
    The sheik can easily afford a Rolls-Royce.

    Which conclusion is correct?

    a. Only a sheik can easily afford a Rolls-Royce.
    b. The sheik is not poor.
    c. The sheik owns a Rolls-Royce.

Computers and plastic cards may some day do away with checks, bills, and coins.

11. Will Money Disappear?

1   Do you know someone who gets Social Security checks? Does this person get checks in the mail? Some people don't get checks now. Each month the money goes right to their bank accounts. The government has a computer. And the bank has a computer too. The government computer tells the bank computer to put the money in an account. That's all it takes. No checks, no waiting. The person can go to the bank and take the money out. That's the first time real cash is used.

2   There's a name for this kind of payment. It's called **Electronic Funds Transfer** or **EFT**. **Electronic** means "done by computer." **Funds** means "money." **Transfer** means "move." So EFT means "computers moving money from one bank account to another." Of course computers don't move dollars and coins. They just move numbers.

3   EFT is a growing thing. Today millions of workers get paid this way. These people work for the government. Their pay is put in their banks. Some 500,000 people pay bills without checks. They tell the bank whom to pay and how much. Then the bank moves the money to these accounts.

4   At many banks, you can get cash from a machine. You don't have to wait in line. You don't even have to go inside the bank. The machine is near the entrance. You can get cash at any time of day.

```
┌─ GLOSSARY ──────────────────────────────────────────────┐
│                                                          │
│  computer      A machine that can solve problems fast.   │
│                Example: The computer kept track of the   │
│                space ship.                               │
│                                                          │
│  electronic    Done by electricity or with a computer.   │
│                Example: They played a new electronic     │
│                football game.                            │
│                                                          │
│  government    People who control a country or city.     │
│                Example: The city government consists of  │
│                the mayor and the people who work for     │
│                him or her.                               │
│                                                          │
│  payment       Something paid.                           │
│                Example: He owes a car payment of $100    │
│                each month.                               │
│                                                          │
│  transfer      Move from one place to another.           │
│                Example: Your business may transfer you   │
│                to another city.                          │
│                                                          │
└──────────────────────────────────────────────────────────┘
```

5   To get cash, you use a card. It looks like a credit card. You put the card into the machine. Then you type your own code number and how much cash you want. The machine drops the cash into a drawer. A computer inside the machine is hooked up to your bank. It tells the bank to take the correct amount from your account.

6   Many people own a computer. They may be able to do "at home" banking. Instead of writing checks they use the computer. They type in the amounts and the names of the people they want to pay. Then the computer sends the information to the bank over the telephone. The bank does the rest. Of course, you can't put money into the bank or take cash out with a home computer.

7   Why do we need EFT? Each year 40,000,000,000 (billion) checks are written. People have to write each check and mail it. Someone else opens the envelope and puts the check in the bank. That bank sends it back to the first bank. Then money can be moved. It can go from one account to another. It takes a lot of people to do all this work. It takes a lot of paper, too. Banks and businesses drown in paper.

8   It costs a lot to pay with checks. You pay 10 to 15 cents to write a check. You pay for stamps. Banks pay 13 to 35 cents to their workers for each check. Businesses pay their workers. The whole cost is $10,000,000,000 (billion) a year.

9   EFT cuts down costs. It skips a lot of steps. Money is moved right away. Almost no paper is needed. In 20 years we may use EFT for everything. In fact it may be impossible to use money at all. It may disappear.

Reading Skills BOOK 2
SELECTION 11

1. What may EFT do?

    a. replace cash and checks
    b. replace computers
    c. replace newspapers

2. EFT stands for

    a. easy fast transfer
    b. electronic funds transfer
    c. only the computer knows

3. EFT

    a. is not used yet
    b. was used 100 years ago
    c. is used now

4. (Paragraph 1) How does the government move Social Security money to someone's bank account?

    a. it puts the money in a car and drives over
    b. one computer tells another to move the money
    c. it mails a check to the bank

5. (Paragraph 5) When you get cash from a machine, how does your bank find out how much you got?

    a. a computer inside the machine notifies your bank
    b. a bank officer notifies your bank
    c. you notify your bank

6. (Paragraph 7) How many checks are written each year?

    a. 10,000,000,000
    b. 40,000,000,000
    c. 1,000,000,000

7. (Paragraph 6) If you do "at home" banking with a computer, you can

    a. deposit money
    b. get cash
    c. pay bills

8. Why does EFT cost less than checks?

   a. computers are cheap
   b. more steps are needed with EFT
   c. many steps are skipped with EFT

9. Why do you need a secret code number with an EFT Card?

   a. so no one else can use your card
   b. to tell the computer how much money you have
   c. because the computer likes numbers

10. If we used EFT for everything and you lost your card

   a. you would go to jail
   b. you'd be in big trouble
   c. no one would care

Vocabulary Skills BOOK 2 SELECTION 11

Glossary Check. Find the Glossary word that should go in each sentence. Then write the word in the space provided.

   1. On April 15 most people who owe taxes make a_____ .

   2. A _____ can handle numbers faster than people.

Word Meanings. The meaning of a word depends on how the word is used.

   3. Paragraph 1 says:
   "Each month the money goes right to their bank accounts."

   In this sentence, what does **account** mean?

   a. explain
   b. story
   c. record

   4. Paragraph 3 says:
   "Their pay is put in their banks."

   In this sentence, what does **pay** mean?

   a. money received from work
   b. hand money to someone
   c. make a visit

5. Paragraph 4 says:

   "The machine is hooked up to the bank."

   In this sentence, what does **hooked** mean?

   a. bent
   b. connected
   c. caught

6. Paragraph 5 says:

   "The machine drops the cash into a drawer."

   Write the word that means **money**.

7. Paragraph 8 says:

   "It costs a lot to pay with checks."

   Write the word that means **slips of paper that stand for money**.

8. Paragraph 9 says:

   "It skips a lot of steps."

   Write the word that means **misses**.

Prefixes. The prefix *im-* often means "not."

Paragraph 9 says:
"In fact it may be impossible to use money at all."

The word **impossible** means "not possible."

The word **impolite** means "not polite."

9. What does **imperfect** means?

   a. more perfect
   b. not perfect
   c. not possible

10. What does **impractical** mean?

    a. in practice
    b. not practical
    c. practical

Thinking Skills BOOK 2 SELECTION 11

Things in Common. Looking at a list of things and seeing what they all have in common is a valuable thinking skill.

1. Look at the following list of words:

    checks   cash   credit cards   EFT

    The best and most complete way to describe these words to someone is to say that they are all

    a. money
    b. things in a bank
    c. ways to pay for things

2. Look at these words:

    banks   law firms   publishing companies   department stores

    Again, which of the following describes all the words best and most completely?

    a. businesses
    b. groups
    c. places that handle money

Definitions. When you define a word, you often have to start off by thinking about what general kind of thing it is.

3. Look at the definition of the word *teller* in the Glossary. It says a teller is a person in a bank.
    What is the best way to describe what general kind of person a *major* is?

    a. someone who fights
    b. someone in the army
    c. someone with a uniform

4. What is the best way to describe what general kind of thing *coins* are?

    a. money
    b. silver
    c. when someone asks you to pay

5. A definition often starts out with telling something general. Then it goes on to give more information about the word.

    Look at the definition of *computer* in the Glossary. Then look at this definition:

    calculator   A machine . . .

    This definition is incomplete. The best way to complete it would be to add the words

    a. made of plastic and metal
    b. that does arithmetic
    c. that you press buttons to make it work

You can get more stations on your radio at night than in the daytime. The reason may surprise you.

12. Hearing Far-Off Radio Stations at Night

1   It's night time. You're driving along in your car. The radio is turned on. But you don't like what it's playing. So you tune in on another station. You move the dial back and forth. You want to get something you like.

2   Finally you tune in on a good song. It's not as loud as you'd like. But it's loud enough to listen to. You stick with the station a while. Then the announcer comes on. He gives the name of the station. It's over 500 miles away!

3   You never picked up this station in the daytime. How can you get it at night?

4   The answer comes from the way radio waves travel. The waves from a radio station travel in two ways. Some of the waves go out straight. They travel along the ground. They go out for about 100 miles. Then they lose their strength. These "ground" waves are the ones your set usually picks up. But you lose them when you're more than 100 miles from the station.

5   The other radio waves don't stick to the ground. They go up into the sky. But they don't keep going. They hit a special layer of air. This air has an electric charge. The radio waves can't go through the charged air. They bounce off it. This sends them back to earth again.

6   In the daytime, the layer of charged air is close to the ground. The radio waves don't bounce far. But at night, the layer is much higher up. The radio waves bounce much farther.

┌─ **GLOSSARY** ───┐

announcer	Someone who talks on a radio or a TV program. ***Example:*** The radio announcer read the news report.
dial	A knob on a radio. ***Example:*** Bill turned the dial to get another station.
electric charge	An amount of electricity. ***Example:*** Your car battery needs an electric charge.
radio waves	The radio signals sent through the air. ***Example:*** Radio waves go hundreds of miles before they fade away.

└──┘

7   It's like bouncing a ball off a ceiling. If the ceiling is low, the ball can't go far. It hits the ground too soon. But if the ceiling is high, the ball will go a lot farther.

8   At night, the radio waves bounce off this high layer of charged air. They may even bounce two or three times between the earth and the sky. They can go long distances this way. They can go much farther from the station than the ground waves can.

9   And your radio set picks them up. With luck, you can listen to the station all night long. That is, if you stay up all night.

10   Then the sun rises. The charged air layer moves in closer to the earth. And you can no longer hear the far-off station. You have to wait until night to hear it again.

Reading Skills BOOK 2
SELECTION 12

1. What are the two kinds of radio waves called?

    a. ground waves and sky waves
    b. high waves and low waves
    c. in waves and out waves

2. What happens to sky waves?

    a. they bounce back to earth
    b. they disappear
    c. they go out into space

3. When you hear a far-off radio station at night, you have picked up

    a. ground waves
    b. sky waves
    c. X-rays

4. (Paragraph 4) How far do ground waves usually go?

    a. 1 mile
    b. 10 miles
    c. 100 miles

5. (Paragraph 6) The layer of charged air is highest

    a. at night
    b. in the daytime
    c. in the winter

6. Radio sky waves bounce farthest when the charged layer of air is

    a. high
    b. near the ground
    c. under the ground

7. The charged layer of air acts like

    a. a ceiling
    b. a floor
    c. a wall

8. What happens to the charged layer of air when the sun rises?

    a. it disappears
    b. it moves closer
    c. it moves farther away

9. Suppose the sky did **not** have a charged layer of air. What do you think would happen?

    a. radio waves would bounce farther
    b. we could never hear far-off radio stations
    c. we would hear far-off stations better

10. What do you think makes the charged layer of air move up and down each day?

    a. the radio set
    b. the radio station
    c. the sun

Vocabulary Skills BOOK 2
SELECTION 12

Glossary Check. Find the Glossary word that should go in each sentence. Then write the word.

1. Julie shut off the radio by turning a _____.

2. I love to listen to that program because I like the voice of the _____.

Word Meanings. The meaning of a word depends on how the word is used.

3. Paragraph 2 says:
    "Finally you tune in on a good song."

    In this sentence, what does **tune** mean?

    a. fix a guitar so it plays on key
    b. song
    c. turn the dial

4. Paragraph 4 says:
    "These 'ground' waves are the ones your set usually picks up."

    In this sentence, what does **set** mean?

    a. group of people
    b. place
    c. radio

5. Paragraph 5 says:

   "The radio waves can't go through the charged air."

   In this sentence, what does **charged** mean?

   a. attacked
   b. cost money
   c. filled with electricity

6. Paragraph 7 says:

   "It's like bouncing a ball off a ceiling."

   Write the word that means **top of a room**.

7. Paragraph 10 says:

   "The charged air layer moves in closer to the earth."

   Write the word that means **nearer**.

8. Paragraph 4 says:

   "Some of the waves go out straight. They travel along the ground."

   This time, write the word that means the <u>opposite</u> of **crooked**.

Alphabetical Order. To put words in alphabetical, or a-b-c order, look at the first letters of the words. These words are in alphabetical order:

1. back	2. may	3. today
car	might	took
full	more	town

9. Which word would you put next after the word **radio**?

   a. reach
   b. rope
   c. run

10. Look again at the words in question 9. Which word would you put next after the word **rises**?

Thinking Skills BOOK 2 SELECTION 12

Correct Order. Putting things in correct order is an important thinking skill.

1. Look at the list below. Put the items in order of <u>distance</u>, from shortest to farthest.
   (1 = shortest, 2 = farther, 3 = farthest)

   a. ___ distance a ground wave travels
   b. ___ distance a radio wave can travel at night
   c. ___ distance you can walk in an hour

2. Look at the list. Put the items in order of <u>height</u>, from lowest to highest.
   (1 = lowest, 2 = next higher, 3 = highest)

   a. ___ height of charged layer of air at night
   b. ___ height of charged layer of air in the daytime
   c. ___ your height

3. Look at the list. Put the items in order of <u>speed</u>, from slowest to fastest.
   (1 = slowest, 2 = faster, 3 = fastest)

   a. ___ speed of a radio wave
   b. ___ speed of a fastball in baseball
   c. ___ your top running speed

Cause and Effect. Look at these two sentences:

Billie told a joke. Everybody laughed.

Telling a joke caused everybody to laugh. The telling is the **cause**. Everybody laughing is the **effect**. We say that the two sentences show a **cause-effect** relationship.

4. Check the pair of sentences below that have a cause-effect relationship in the story. (The first is the reason for the second, or causes the second.)

   a. At night, the layer of charged air is higher up. The radio waves bounce much farther.
   b. You can listen all night. That is, if you stay up all night.
   c. You tune in on a good song. It's not as loud as you'd like.

5. Again, check the pair of sentences that have a cause-effect relationship.

   a. At night you can hear far-off radio stations. During the day, you can't.
   b. The sun rises. The charged air layer moves in closer to the earth.
   c. The waves from a radio station travel in two ways. Some go out straight.

The case of Clarence Gideon, who was sent to jail because he didn't have a lawyer to defend him.

13. The Drifter Who Changed the Law

1   On the night of June 3, 1961, a pool hall in a small Florida town was robbed. The police soon picked up the man they thought did it. He was a poor drifter. He went from town to town gambling. His name was Clarence Earl Gideon. He said he didn't do it. But he had a record. After a short trial, he was sent to jail.

2   The case should have stopped there. But it didn't. Gideon felt he had been treated unfairly. Since he was poor, he had no lawyer at his trial. So he wrote to the Supreme Court of the United States.

3   Now the Supreme Court gets a great many letters. Some are from nuts. But this letter touched on a basic question. No man should be sent to jail without a fair trial. The Supreme Court decided to look into his case.

4   The Court had looked at a case like this 20 years before. At that time it had said a man had to pay for his lawyer. If he was too poor, he was out of luck. He could only get a lawyer free if his was a special case. And Gideon's case was not special.

5   Gideon asked the Court to change its mind. As he wrote, "It makes no difference how old I am or what color I am. The question is I did not get a fair trial."

GLOSSARY

drifter	A person who moves a lot from place to place. *Example:* A drifter never holds a job for long.
gambling	Betting on games and sports. *Example:* Betting on horse races is a kind of gambling.
guilty	Having broken a law. *Example:* At the trial, the man was found guilty of stealing a car.
record	A police list of a person's crimes. *Example:* Someone who has been in prison many times has a long record.
Supreme Court	The most powerful court in the U.S. *Example:* The Supreme Court can often change what other courts say or do.

---

6   The Court heard opinions from fine lawyers in all parts of the country. Finally it made a decision. It had changed its mind. The old rule was dead. Now every man on trial for a serious crime had to be given a lawyer. It did not matter whether he was too poor to pay. Gideon was to have a new trial. And he was to get a lawyer, free of charge.

7   But Gideon was stubborn to the end. He said he did not want a new trial. He wanted to be set free. He said he did not want a lawyer after all. But he got one anyway. And he was tried again. This time, he was found not guilty. He left the prison a free man.

8   He fought when he thought he was right. And the highest court in the land took the time to listen. A law that affected millions of people was changed. And all because a stubborn man sat down one day to write to the Supreme Court.

Reading Skills BOOK 2
SELECTION 13

1. How did Gideon get the law changed?

    a. he wrote to Congress
    b. he wrote to the President
    c. he wrote to the Supreme Court

2. Why did Gideon feel he was treated unfairly?

    a. he didn't have a lawyer
    b. the judge was crooked
    c. the jury had been bribed

3. What finally happened to Gideon?

    a. he was given a life sentence
    b. he was sent back to jail
    c. he was set free after a new trial

4. (Paragraph 1) Gideon was tried for

    a. drifting
    b. gambling
    c. robbery

5. (Paragraph 6) The Supreme Court said that

    a. Gideon was right
    b. Gideon was wrong
    c. they didn't want to hear anything about it

6. Earlier, the Supreme Court had said that

    a. every man gets a lawyer for free
    b. a man has to pay for a lawyer
    c. no man is allowed to have a lawyer

7. The Supreme Court

    a. changed its mind on the Gideon case
    b. did not change its mind in the Gideon case
    c. set Gideon free

8. Today, every poor man on trial for a serious crime gets

   a. a jail sentence
   b. a lawyer to help him for free
   c. set free

9. The Supreme Court listened to lawyers from all over the country. What do you think most of the lawyers said?

   a. forget about the case—Gideon isn't important
   b. Gideon should not be given a lawyer
   c. Gideon should be given a lawyer

10. Gideon was

    a. a good family man
    b. a good worker
    c. stubborn

Vocabulary Skills BOOK 2
SELECTION 13

Glossary Check. Find the Glossary word that should go in each sentence. Then write the word.

1. Playing poker is a kind of _____.

2. Someone who thinks his or her trial was unfair sometimes takes the case to the _____.

Word Meanings. The meaning of a word depends on how the word is used.

3. Paragraph 1 says:
   "...a pool hall in a small Florida town was robbed."

   In this sentence, what does **pool** mean?

   a. game
   b. small lake
   c. water

4. Paragraph 3 says:
   "Some are from nuts."

   In this sentence, what does **nuts** mean?

   a. crazy people
   b. something to eat
   c. something used in a tool shop

5. Paragraph 5 says:

   "Gideon asked the Court to change its mind."

   In this sentence, what does *mind* mean?

   a. care
   b. decision
   c. do as you are told

6. Paragraph 2 says:

   "Gideon felt he had been treated unfairly."

   Write the word that means *thought*.

7. Paragraph 6 says:

   "The old rule was dead."

   Write the word that means *law*.

8. Paragraph 6 says:

   "It had changed its mind. The old rule was dead."

   This time, write the word that means the <u>opposite</u> of *alive*.

Prefixes. The prefix *un-* often means "not..."

Paragraph 2 says: "Gideon felt he had been treated unfairly."

The word *unfairly* means "not fairly."

The word *unkind* means "not kind."

9. What does *unwise* mean?

   a. most wise
   b. not wise
   c. wiser

10. What does *untrue* mean?

    a. false
    b. more true
    c. not blue

Thinking Skills BOOK 2
SELECTION 13

Fact and Opinion. In your thinking, you should be able to tell a fact from an opinion.

"The sun is a star" is a *fact*. It can be proved by a scientist.
"George Washington was a great president" is an *opinion*. It may be a good opinion, but it's not something a scientist can prove.

1. Which of these statements states a *fact*? (choose one)

   a. Gideon asked the court to change its mind.
   b. "It makes no difference how old I am or what color I am."
   c. "I did not get a fair trial."

2. Which of these statements states an *opinion*? (choose one)

   a. Gideon was treated unfairly.
   b. He had no lawyer at his trial.
   c. He wrote to the Supreme Court.

Logical Thinking. Thinking logically means taking information and drawing the right conclusions from it.

3. Look at these statements:

   Some drifters sometimes commit crimes.
   Gideon was a drifter.

   Which conclusion is correct?

   a. Gideon committed crimes and was guilty of the robbery.
   b. Gideon did not commit crimes and was innocent of the robbery.
   c. Neither conclusion is correct from the information given.

4. Look at these statements:

   No man should be sent to jail without a fair trial.
   Gideon did not get a fair trial.

   Which conclusion is correct?

   a. Gideon should have been sent to jail.
   b. Gideon should not have been sent to jail.
   c. Neither conclusion is correct from the information given.

5. Look at these statements:

   Some letters to the Supreme Court are from nuts.
   Gideon wrote a letter to the Supreme Court.

   Which conclusion is correct?

   a. Gideon was a nut.
   b. Gideon was not a nut.
   c. Neither conclusion is correct from the information given.

Columbus arrived in the New World in 1492. That's almost 500 years too late for him to be the true European discoverer of America.

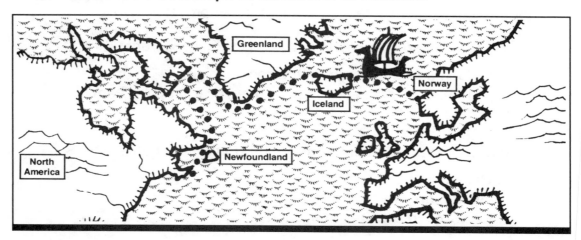

14. Who Discovered America?

1   Who was the first European to discover America? Do you think it was Columbus? Many people don't think so. They think the Vikings got here first. A coin found in Maine helps show that they may be right.

2   The coin is the size of a dime. It is silver and has a cross on one side. There is an animal head on the other side. The coin was found in an old rubbish heap in Blue Hill, Maine. The heap was left over from an old Indian village. A man found the coin in 1961. Everyone thought it was an old English coin. They thought that it was 600 years old.

3   One man did not think the coin was English. In 1978 he took a picture of the coin. He brought it to England. He asked a coin expert to look at it. The expert said, "It's not an English coin." He said it was a penny from Norway. Others said so too. They said it was made about 1075.

4   How did the coin get to Maine? Well, the Vikings may have brought it. The Vikings were sailors from what is now Norway, Sweden, and Denmark. They were also pirates, traders, and explorers. They may have been in Maine around 1075.

5   The Vikings were good sailors. Their ships were large. Many were between 100 and 150 feet long. They were long and thin. They could hold more than 50 people. The bow of the ship was carved to look like the head of a dragon. The Vikings were able to sail these ships a long way. They knew how to steer by the stars. They knew how to cross the open sea.

GLOSSARY

exist	To be real; to live. *Example:* My little brother thinks ghosts exist.
fierce	Strong and wild; frightening. *Example:* Tigers are fierce.
bow	Front of a ship. *Example:* He stood in the bow of the boat and looked for land.
rubbish	Garbage; litter. *Example:* They cleaned the garage and put the rubbish out to be taken away.

---

6   Old stories tell us that the Vikings sailed to Iceland. From there they sailed to Greenland. They got to Greenland in the year 986. We have found Viking houses there. Then the Vikings sailed to a place they called Vinland.

7   The Vikings came to Vinland many times. One year, 160 people came in three ships. But there were other people in Vinland. They were fierce. The Vikings had to leave.

8   For years no one knew where Vinland was. Some thought it did not exist. They thought it was just a story. But some thought it could be part of North America.

9   Some time ago an old town was found. It was found in Newfoundland, a part of Canada. Eight houses were dug up. The town was built around the year 1000. It may have been Vinland.

10   What about the coin? Did the Vikings come to Maine too? There is no other sign that they did. No other Viking objects have been found. Maybe an Indian brought the coin. The Indians from Newfoundland were good sailors too. Did one of them bring the coin to Maine?

11   The coin may have been left in Maine by the Vikings. It may have been brought there by Indians. We do not know. But the coin shows that Vikings were near Maine. It tells us that Vikings were in North America in the 11th century. That is 400 years before Columbus.

12   Who discovered America? We don't know. The Indians were here thousands of years before the Vikings. They were here long before Columbus. But the first Europeans to come here may have been the Vikings.

Reading Skills BOOK 2
SELECTION 14

1. Who probably came to America first?

   a. Columbus
   b. the English
   c. the Vikings

2. Vikings were able to sail

   a. only short distances
   b. only on lakes
   c. on the open seas

3. The coin found in Maine

   a. gives clues about who discovered America
   b. is an English penny
   c. is a fake

4. (Paragraph 2) When was the coin found?

   a. 600
   b. 1961
   c. 1492

5. (Paragraph 5) What was on the bow of a Viking ship?

   a. a dragon's head
   b. a Viking
   c. an Indian

6. (Paragraph 6) The Vikings first sailed to

   a. Norway
   b. Greenland
   c. Iceland

7. The coin is a penny from

   a. Norway
   b. Maine
   c. England

8. Who could have brought the coin to Maine?

   a. the English
   b. Indians or Vikings
   c. dragons

9. The Vikings lived

   a. near the sea
   b. far from the sea
   c. in the desert

10. The fierce people in Vinland may have been

    a. Vikings
    b. Columbus
    c. Indians

Vocabulary Skills BOOK 2 SELECTION 14

Glossary Check. Find the Glossary word that should go in each sentence. Then write the word.

1. Tigers in cages are not as _____ as wild ones.

2. Some people litter the roads with _____.

Word Meanings. The meaning of a word depends on how the word is used.

3. Paragraph 5 says:
   "The bow of the ship was carved to look like the head of a dragon."

   In this sentence, what does **bow** mean?

   a. bend over
   b. fancy knot
   c. front of a boat

4. Paragraph 5 says:
   "They were long and thin."

   In this sentence, what does **thin** mean?

   a. narrow
   b. under weight
   c. tall

5. Paragraph 7 says:
   "The Vikings had to leave."

   In this sentence, what does **leave** mean?

   a. go away
   b. let go
   c. part of a tree

6. Paragraph 7 says:

"The Vikings came to Vinland many times."

Write the word that means **more than one**.

7. Paragraph 12 says:

"Who discovered America?"

Write the word that means **found**.

8. Paragraph 1 says:

"They think the Vikings got here first."

This time, write the word that means the <u>opposite</u> of **last**.

Using Apostrophes. The meaning of a word or a sentence may depend on how apostrophes are used.

9. Paragraph 5 says:

"The bow of the ship was carved to look like the head of a dragon."

What is another way to write **head of a dragon**?

a. dragon head's
b. dragon's head
c. heady dragon

10. Paragraph 3 says:

The expert said, "It's not an English coin."

What is another way to write **It's not**?

a. It did not
b. The not of it
c. It is not

Thinking Skills BOOK 2 SELECTION 14

Correct Order. Putting things in correct order is an important thinking skill.

1. Look at the list below. Put the items in order of <u>time</u>, from earliest to latest.

(1 = earliest, 2 = later, 3 = latest)

a. ___ date of coin found in Maine
b. ___ date of Viking town in Newfoundland
c. ___ Vikings discover Greenland

2. Look at the list. Again, put the items in order of <u>time</u>, from earliest to latest.

   a. ___ Columbus comes to America
   b. ___ Indians come to America
   c. ___ Vikings come to America

3. Look at the list. Put the places in order of <u>distance</u> from the Viking's homeland of Norway, from closest to farthest away.

   a. ___ Greenland
   b. ___ Iceland
   c. ___ Newfoundland

Cause and Effect. Look at these two sentences:

   Billie told a joke. Everybody laughed.

Telling a joke caused everybody to laugh. The telling is the *cause*. Everybody laughing is the *effect*. We say that the two sentences show a *cause-effect* relationship.

4. Check the pair of sentences below that have a cause-effect relationship in the story. (The first is the reason for the second, or causes the second.)

   a. The Vikings came to Vinland many times. One year, 360 people came.
   b. The Vikings learned to steer by the stars. They started crossing the open sea.
   c. The Vikings were good sailors. Their ships were long and thin.

5. Again, check the pair of sentences that have a cause-effect relationship.

   a. There were fierce people in Vinland. The Vikings had to leave.
   b. No one knew where Vinland was. Some people thought it could be in North America.
   c. Some years ago a Viking town was found. It was found in Newfoundland.

89

The Bible story of the strongman who pulled down a building with his bare hands.

15. The Temple Fell

1   Have you ever heard of Samson? He was one of the great heroes of the Bible. No man could match his strength. He could kill a lion with his bare hands. And once he got mad and killed a thousand men who tried to kill him.

2   Samson was an Israelite. At that time his land was ruled by men called Philistines. The Philistines did not mind when Samson killed lions. But they did mind when he killed Philistines. And Samson killed *only* Philistines.

3   The Philistines tried more than once to get hold of Samson. But each time he was caught, he got away. Samson was just too strong.

4   Then Samson met Delilah. Samson could kill many men. But Delilah was a beautiful woman. One look at Delilah and Samson would melt.

5   Now Delilah knew there was a secret to Samson's strength. And the Philistines would pay a lot to know that secret. Delilah decided to make Samson talk.

6   Samson knew he should not trust Delilah. And yet he could not stay away from her. And at last he told her his secret. "It's my hair, Delilah," he said. "I've never cut it. If my hair were cut, I'd lose my strength."

7   "I won't tell a soul," whispered Delilah. And right away she sent for the Philistines.

8   That afternoon, Samson fell asleep on Delilah's lap. Delilah shaved off all his hair. Then she whispered in his ear, "Get up! The Philistines are here!"

GLOSSARY

column	One of the stone or wood posts that holds up a building. *Example:* If you tear down that column, the roof will fall in.
Israelites	The early Jews. *Example:* The Israelites lived thousands of years ago.
Philistines	A people who ruled part of Israel in the early days. *Example:* The Israelites hated the Philistines.
temple	A kind of church. *Example:* The people went to the temple to pray.

---

9   Samson jumped up and charged at the Philistines. But without his hair, he was too weak to fight. The Philistines tied him up. They put out both his eyes. And then they threw him into jail.

10   Blind and weak, Samson lay in jail. He prayed for a chance to get even. Slowly his hair began to grow back. And finally his chance came.

11   The Philistines held a big party in one of their temples. After a while they sent for Samson. They wanted to make fun of the Israelite "strong man."

12   A small boy led Samson into the temple. He left Samson by two large columns that held up the roof. Samson could hear the Philistines as they laughed at him.

13   Samson ran his fingers through his short hair. Then he grabbed the two columns. "Please, God," he prayed. "Give me back my strength. Just for one minute. Let me pay them back for my eyes!"

14   Samson pulled on the columns with all his might. At first nothing happened. Then the columns gave way. The whole temple caved in.

15   Samson was killed. But 3,000 of the hated Philistines died with him.

Reading Skills BOOK 2
SELECTION 15

1. What made the temple fall?

   a. an earthquake made it fall down
   b. a strong man pulled it down
   c. it was built badly, and fell down by itself

2. Whose temple was it?

   a. the Israelites' temple
   b. the Philistines' temple
   c. Samson's temple

3. Samson was strong because

   a. he came from a family of strong men
   b. he exercised a lot
   c. he had long hair

4. (Paragraph 1) This story comes from

   a. American history
   b. the Bible
   c. a poem

5. (Paragraph 8) What did Delilah do to make Samson weak?

   a. she broke his arms
   b. she poisoned him
   c. she shaved off his hair

6. (Paragraph 9) What did the Philistines do to Samson when they caught him?

   a. they didn't do anything to him
   b. they put out both his eyes
   c. they threw him to the lions

7. Who was Delilah?

   a. a woman Samson loved
   b. an Israelite hero
   c. a Philistine soldier

8. How did Samson get his strength back?

    a. he got his sight back
    b. he worked out with weights
    c. his hair grew back

9. What kind of woman was Delilah?

    a. the kind to stay away from
    b. the kind you can trust
    c. the kind who would make a good wife

10. If Samson were alive today, what job would be best for him?

    a. barber
    b. Rock and Roll singer
    c. strong man in the movies

Vocabulary Skills BOOK 2 SELECTION 15

Glossary Check. Find the Glossary word that should go in each sentence. Then write the word.

1. The steps led up into a large _____.

2. That building has strong enough walls to hold up the roof. I don't see why they put in that _____.

Word Meanings. The meaning of a word depends on how the word is used.

3. Paragraph 2 says:
"At that time his land was ruled by men called Philistines."

    In this sentence, what does *land* mean?

    a. country
    b. earth
    c. ground

4. Paragraph 7 says:
"'I won't tell a soul,' whispered Delilah."

    In this sentence, what does *soul* mean?

    a. feeling
    b. person
    c. spirit

5. Paragraph 14 says:

   "Samson pulled on the columns with all his might."

   In this sentence, what does *might* mean?

   a. could
   b. may be able
   c. strength

6. Paragraph 1 says:

   "And once he got mad and killed a thousand men."

   Write the word that means *angry*.

7. Paragraph 2 says:

   "The Philistines did not mind when Samson killed lions."

   Write the word that means *care*.

8. Paragraph 8 says:

   "Then she whispered in his ear, 'Get up! The Philistines are here!'"

   This time, write the word that means the <u>opposite</u> of *shouted*.

Suffixes. The suffix *-ly* often means "in a . . . way."

Paragraph 10 says: "Slowly his hair began to grow back."

The word *slowly* means "in a slow way."

The word *strongly* means "in a strong way."

9. What does *happily* mean?

   a. happier
   b. in a baggy way
   c. in a happy way

10. What does *softly* mean?

    a. in a hard way
    b. in a soft way
    c. most soft

Thinking Skills BOOK 2
SELECTION 15

Things in Common. Looking at a list of things and seeing what they all have in common is a valuable thinking skill.

1. Look at the following list of words:

      Samson   Delilah   Adam   Eve

The best and most complete way to describe these words to someone is to say that they are all

a. men and women
b. names
c. people in the Bible

2. Look at these words:

      shave   cut   clip   trim

Again, which of the following describes all the words best and most completely?

a. ways to give shape to trees and bushes
b. ways to make hair shorter or get rid of it
c. what Delilah did to Samson

Definitions. When you define a word, you often have to start off by thinking about what general kind of thing it is.

3. Look at the definition of the word **column** in the Glossary. It says a column in a post.
What is the best way to describe what general kind of thing a **roof** is?

a. a covering
b. my house has one
c. stone or wood

4. What is the best way to describe what kind of thing a **doorway** is?

a. houses and buildings have them
b. an opening
c. when you go through it

5. A definition often starts out with telling something general. Then it goes on to give more information about the word.

Look at the definition of **Philistine** in the Glossary. Then look at this definition:

     Apaches An Indian people . . .

This definition is incomplete. The best way to complete it would be to add the words

a. of the southwestern United States
b. who often had long hair
c. who were native to America